COACHING

Richard
W.
Harvey

BASKETBALL'S

MULTIPLE SET

ZONE OFFENSE

PARKER PUBLISHING COMPANY, INC.
West Nyack, N.Y.

©1973 *by*

Parker Publishing Company, Inc.

West Nyack, N.Y.

*All rights reserved. No part of this
book may be reproduced in any form
or by any means without permission
in writing from the publisher.*

Library of Congress Cataloging in Publication Data

Harvey, Richard W   (date)
   Coaching basketball's multiple set zone offense.

   1. Basketball coaching. I. Title.
GV885.3.H37   796.32'3'077   72-10108
ISBN 0-13-139287-5

Printed in the United States of America

Why I Wrote This Book and How It Will Help You

Coaching Basketball's Multiple Set Zone Offense was written with a specific purpose in mind, that of concentrating entirely on the concept of defeating zone and situation defenses. Approximately 85-90% of our basketball games each season are played against some version of a zone defense. It would not be surprising if that percentage exists in high school basketball in many areas. The material in this book will be geared to building a consistent offense to adjust to all of the problems presented by straight, variation, and pressure zone defenses.

The concept of zone defense is becoming increasingly prominent as the major form of defensive basketball strategy on the high school level. Most high school basketball teams possess only one or two consistent outside shooters who are capable of scoring from long range. Therefore, the zone defense or variation has become the most successful means of neutralizing offensive scoring ability. In addition, a zone defense also provides good protection against fouling and maintains good rebounding strength to initiate fast break opportunities.

One section of this book will be devoted to analyzing the various zone defenses that will be encountered and the methods of creating offensive pressure to defeat them. The concepts presented have been used successfully in our basketball program. In terms of readiness, we have never entered a game in which our team was not able to cope with the type of defense employed against us.

Oftentimes the offensive philosophy used against a zone defense revolves around the ability of a team to convert a high

4 *Why I Wrote This Book and How It Will Help You*

percentage of their shots from the outside over the zone. Consequently, a "hot" shooting night would result in a win whereas a "cold" shooting night would result in a loss. A percentage situation such as this simply becomes a shooting contest and will result in a losing basketball program in the long run.

Another section will be devoted to analyzing the weak points of the various zone defenses and to examine both inside and perimeter attacks to develop a consistent scoring offense. Information pertaining to shooting techniques will be discussed and drills specific to securing the good percentage shots will be presented.

The zone defense is becoming highly sophisticated. Many zones are geared to applying pressure on the ball, on a specific player, or on a specific area of the court rather than relying on the conventional shifts originally intended for each specific zone. An analysis of the specific options to be employed to prevent the corner trap, sideline force, double-up situations, and other forms of pressure to disrupt the offensive tempo will be covered. There are also zone automatic maneuvers such as the cut and reverse, fake and penetrate, and reversing the pass which when utilized properly will develop a successful scoring attack.

A major problem presented by the zone defense concerns the area of player confidence. Lack of confidence may be developed in the players if they are not adequately prepared to meet all zone situations. Therefore, offensive ideas and patterns to combat the zone presses and situation defenses such as the box and one, diamond and one, and triangle and two will be developed.

The basis upon which the multiple set zone offense was developed was to prepare our players with the necessary tools to cope with the various forms of zone defenses encountered. The system is based on flexibility and execution. After the original patterns are developed, only minor adjustments of player placement are needed to instill in the players the confidence needed to attack and defeat zones. The multiple set zone offense incorporates five basic sets. These are a 1-3-1, 2-1-2, 2-2-1, 3-2, and 1-3-1 overload. A thorough discussion on the development of these patterns into a unit are necessary to gain insight in offensive strategy against zone defenses.

Why I Wrote This Book and How It Will Help You 5

We have employed the multiple set system each year making only minor adjustments due to changing personnel and experience. It provides the players with a thorough knowledge of the offensive principles in attacking zones along with stimulating them to become thinking basketball players.

Dick Harvey

Contents

1. Advantages and Principles of the Multiple Set Zone Offense • 13

Developing Zone Awareness
Developing Player Confidence
Developing Positional Strengths
Developing an Offensive Advantage
Adjusting to Changing Defenses
Incorporating Player Continuity
Rotating the Pattern
Overloading an Area
Penetrating the Defense
Spreading the Defense
Passing and Moving
Developing Variation in the Offensive Attack
Disrupting Defensive Plans
Utilizing Individual Strengths
Forcing a Defensive Commitment

**2. Developing Offensive Pressure with the Multiple Set
Zone Offense • 23**

Creating a Mismatch
Utilizing Passing Triangles
Splitting the Defense
Employing Weakside Action
Screening the Zone
Committing the Defense

2. Developing Offensive Pressure with the Multiple Set Zone Offense (cont.)

Penetrating on a Dribble
Overloading a Side
Emphasizing Pattern Execution

3. The Basic Positions in the Multiple Set Zone Offense • 35

Player Analysis
Player Positions

1. The Point Position
2. The High Post Position
3. The Low Post Position
4. The Wing Position
5. The Double Guard Positions
6. The Double Low Post Positions

4. Developing an Interior Attack with the Multiple Set Zone Offense • 47

The High Post Options
The Low Post Options
The High Post-Low Post Exchange
The Double Low Post Exchange
The Low Post Loop
The Low Post Roll
The Weakside Sift
The Low Post Flash
The Inside Rotation
Summary

5. The Offensive Patterns in the Multiple Set Zone Offense • 63

The 1-3-1 Cut and Roll Set
The 2-1-2 Perimeter Set
The 3-2 Baseline Screen Set
The 2-2-1 Weakside Slide Set
The 1-3-1 Overload Set
Summary of Principles

6. Automatic Maneuvers in the Multiple Set Zone Offense • 87

Reversing the Pass
Releasing and Moving
Cutting and Reversing
Penetrating the Baseline

Contents   *9*

6. Automatic Maneuvers in the Multiple Set Zone Offense (cont.)

Faking and Penetrating
Shooting and Following

7. Breakdown Drills to Develop the Multiple Set Zone Offense • 99

Perimeter Passing
Offensive Cutting Action
Post Options
Cut and Reverse Maneuver
Reversing the Passing Action
Faking and Penetrating Points
Summary

8. Offensive Strategy of the Multiple Set Zone Offense • 113

Playing for Close Shots
Percentage Shooting
Attacking the Weak Areas of Zones
Controlling the Tempo of the Game
Patience on Offense
Maintaining Floor Balance
Reacting Quickly from Offense to Defense
Overshifting the Defense
Remaining Active on Offense
Emphasizing Offense Efficiency

9. Multiple Set Option Selection Against Situation Zones • 127

Attacking the Corner Trap
Defeating Midcourt Pressure
Opening the Middle Sag
Preventing Passing Lane Denial
Relieving Fronting Pressure on the High Post
Relieving Fronting Pressure on the Low Post
Defeating the Matchup Zone
Attacking the Backline Zone
Attacking the Frontline Zone
Summary

10. Multiple Set Adjustments to Combat Combination Defenses • 143

The Guard Option vs the Box and 1 Defense
The Forward Option vs the Box and 1 Defense
The Guard Option vs the Diamond and 1 Defense

10. **Multiple Set Adjustments to Combat Combination Defenses (cont.)**

The Forward Option vs the Diamond and 1 Defense
Player Movement Against the Alternating Box and 1 Defense
Double Guard Movement vs the Triangle and 2 Defense
Guard-Forward Movement vs the Triangle and 2 Defense
Double Forward Movement vs the Triangle and 2 Defense
Summary

11. **Developing Shooting and Passing Techniques Against Zone Defenses • 163**

Employing a Shooting Index
Six Pointers to Improve Outside Shooting Against Zone Defenses
Shooting Drills

1. Quick Release Drill
2. Pass and Press Drill
3. Around the Horn
4. Spot Shooting Drill
5. Contact Drill
6. 5-10-15 Drill
7. Aggressive Layup Drill
8. Down the Middle Layup Drill
9. Loose Ball Layup Drill
10. Double Team Layup Drill
11. Jumping Layup Drill
12. Two Men Tapping Drill
13. Airborne Layup Drill

Passing Drills

14. Two on One Drill
15. Perimeter Passing Drill
16. Zig Zag Passing Drill
17. Man in the Middle Passing Drill
18. Split the Offense

12. **Attacking Pressure Zones with the Multiple Set Zone Offense • 183**

Analyzing Pressure Situations
Attacking Full Court Zone Pressure
Attacking Three-Quarter Court Zone Pressure

1. 1-3-1 vs 2-2-1 press
2. 1-3-1 vs 2-1-2 Press

Contents 11

12. Attacking Pressure Zones with the Multiple Set Zone Offense (cont.)

3. 2-2-1 vs 1-3-1 Press

Attacking Half Court Zone Pressure

13. Additional Considerations in Instituting the Multiple Set Zone Offense • 201

Evaluation of Personnel
Set Formation
Implication of Statistics
Terminology
Game Strategy
Practice Guidelines

Index • 211

CHAPTER ONE

Advantages and Principles of the Multiple Set Zone Offense

The influence of zone defensive theory and the increase each year in the percentage of teams playing zone defenses has necessitated the importance of creating offensive zone flexibility in high school basketball. With increased television coverage of college basketball games, a greater exposure to the various forms of zone defenses can be seen. Many different types of zone defenses can be observed with different teams and in different areas of the country. The reasons for the increase in number of teams employing a zone defense include:

1. A zone defense is easier and less time consuming to teach effectively than a man for man defense.
2. A zone defense allows constant rebounding position.
3. A zone defense allows a team to protect a star player from getting into serious foul trouble.
4. A zone defense is excellent for initiating the fast break after a rebound.
5. A zone defense utilizes big men better by keeping them around the basket.

14   Advantages and Principles of the Multiple Set Zone Offense

6. A zone defense allows a team to concentrate more on their offensive ability.
7. A zone defense enables a team to control the tempo of the game more consistently.
8. A zone defense is most effective against a poor outside shooting team.
9. A zone defense generally decreases the number of fouls committed. Therefore, it delays the 1-1 going into effect and allows a team to use fouls to their advantage at the end of the half or game.
10. A zone defense allows players to gamble without being burned and also to grab a breather when they are away from the ball.

Zone defenses are designed to play the ball through specific and strategic positioning of the players. Consequently it is easy to create variations to confuse and upset the opponent. A zone defense is psychologically an awesome sight to the offense when the defensive players keep their arms up and hands active. It can be and is frustrating when offensive movement is nullified. Zone defenses can compensate for the two extremes of possessing either a very tall or extremely short team in an attempt to equalize the team's chances of winning.

DEVELOPING ZONE AWARENESS

Developing zone awareness is an important aspect in formulating an offensive attack. The concept refers to the ability of recognizing different zone defenses, and the inherent strengths and weaknesses to be utilized to best advantage. All variations of zone defenses can be basically broken down into two categories. Zone defenses which operate with a two man front (2-2-1, 2-1-2, 2-3) are considered even front zones. Zone defenses which have a one man front or defensive point (1-3-1, 3-2, 1-2-2, 1-1-3, 1-2-1-1) are considered odd front zones. Oftentimes zone defenses will change their formation each time down the floor. Therefore, it is essential that players are taught to recognize the possible variations or changes. They must also possess the necessary offensive tools to cope with the changing defenses.

Incorporating the multiple set zone offense offers the players the proper selection of offensive sets to utilize their individual ability most effectively. The ability to react is learned in practice by exposing the offense to the various zone defenses employed rather than in a hit or miss fashion in a game when mistakes are costly.

All zone defenses have specific strengths and weaknesses. Due to the fast-paced nature of basketball, at times the coach is unable to convey offensive adjustments quickly and efficiently without distracting the players. Therefore, the players must remain alert and be able to analyze the zone defense on the playing floor. Utilizing the multiple set zone offense allows the players to become aware of the strongest points of attack against the different types of zone defenses encountered.

DEVELOPING PLAYER CONFIDENCE

One of the most important elements in succeeding against zone defenses concerns the area of player confidence. Players must develop confidence in themselves, their coach, and the offensive system. It is my feeling that there is no single offensive pattern which will consistently succeed against all zone defenses. Of course, an over-abundance of talent will make any system extremely effective. In high school it is rare when great talent is available year after year. Therefore, adjustments must be made with the changing personnel.

The multiple set zone offense allows personnel with all levels of ability an opportunity to take advantage of the various sets in attacking all zone defenses effectively. A major purpose of using the multiple set is to give the players experience in facing the different kinds of zone defenses employed. Once the players are given knowledge, experience, and achieve success in combating specific zone defenses through practices and scrimmages, the confidence level of the players will be greatly increased. What can be more discouraging and frustrating to a player when he knows the one offensive pattern used is nullified by a particular zone? A choice of offensive sets adds a change of pace and a different method of attack. It not only builds confidence, but also increases the interest level.

DEVELOPING POSITIONAL STRENGTHS

The proper placing of personnel is important in defeating zone defenses. Each zone defense is structured with certain strengths as well as possessing definite weaknesses. The ability of players to exert their offensive strengths in the weak spots of zone defenses develops a greater offensive thrust.

One category that can readily be observed involves special shooting abilities. Accurate shooting records in practice, preseason scrimmages, and actual games can pay valuable dividends. Shooting strengths of individual players can be analyzed and used to advantage. The five areas including the right corner, left corner, right wing, left wing, and top of key require definitive placing of personnel to take advantage. Shooting statistics also relate the fact that certain players shoot better from one side of the court than the other. A lot has been said about players developing proficiency in shooting from all areas on the court to prevent the defense from overplaying and guiding their movement. This is fine and logical in theory, but when it's time to play the game most players will move to areas designated by personal preference. Unless the information derived from shooting statistics is passed on to the player, he may be unaware of why his shooting percentage is decreasing.

DEVELOPING AN OFFENSIVE ADVANTAGE

The major aim in any offensive pattern is geared to developing a consistent offensive advantage. Without offensive movement the pattern is useless. An offensive advantage is created in a number of ways, all of which should be included to some degree in every pattern. In the first place offensive patterns must utilize a passing option. This is necessary to move the defense out of their base positions and force them to make mistakes on defensive coverage as they react to the movement of the ball. Second, the pattern must be able to create an overload on a defensive player or area. This will open up shooting opportunities and change the complexion of the defensive adjustments. Third, offensive patterns are designed to place players in positions to split the defense and force a commitment to create alternate openings. A fourth important point demands the pattern to allow for individual excellence. This takes the form of individual player movement based on pre-determined automatic maneuvers designed to exploit defensive adjustments. Offensive zone patterns must also include opportunities to create both outside and inside scoring possibilities. A team that experiences a poor shooting night must be able to move inside to secure closer shooting attempts. Conversely, a sagging zone

Advantages and Principles of the Multiple Set Zone Offense   **17**

defense must be opened up with outside shooting. And in the final analysis, the offensive pattern must be based on execution drilled through constant repetition. The multiple set zone offense possesses the above-mentioned qualifications.

ADJUSTING TO CHANGING DEFENSES

Coaching variations have made a great impact in defensive basketball theory. Many methods of changing defensive tactics are used such as the time remaining, score, ahead or behind, made or missed field goal, made or missed foul shot, and the time out period.

The offensive pattern must allow for flexibility, and continuity to mount a continuous offensive thrust. Many times a coach is unable to convey a message to the team during the continuous action of the game. Consequently, oftentimes a player on the floor must control the offensive adjustments. Leadership becomes extremely important for a player having pre-instructed information to make and create adjustments to sustain an effective offensive thrust.

INCORPORATING PLAYER CONTINUITY

An effective offensive pattern must include provisions for player continuity. This type of movement keeps constant pressure on the defense. Continuity of movement opens up opportunities for the offense to capitalize on gambling tactics, attempts to overplay, attempts to trap or double team, and to take advantage of the defense when it is caught out of position. Player continuity develops a continuous offensive action and keeps each player alert and aware of every other teammate on the floor to produce offensive openings.

ROTATING THE PATTERN

This concept implies both rotating the players within an offensive set and rotating the sets depending on the alternating action of the defense. The primary aim of course is to change and create stronger offensive opportunities. Rotation can be inside the defense, through the defense, or outside the defense depending on the option selected. The methods employed include exchanging weakside and strongside with both ball and

18   Advantages and Principles of the Multiple Set Zone Offense

player movement, alternating points of attack, counteracting defensive setups with the proper offensive sets, and creating individual mismatches to exploit particular defensive players or areas.

OVERLOADING AN AREA

Overloading in simple terms implies creating an uneven ratio of offensive players to defensive players in a specific area. Generally a two to one situation can be accomplished in favor of the offense. This applies added pressure on the defense by utilizing personnel to gain an offensive advantage on that specific defender or particular on the floor. Essentially, the overload principle will be effective against a zone defense which normally sags to close off the middle. The two best areas to create an overload situation are in either the corner or wing at the foul line extended. It forces the defense to come out or suffer the consequences of giving a good percentage shot from 15 to 18 feet. The most effective methods in taking advantage of the overload principle include utilizing the best shooters to secure their specialized shots, taking advantage of a player experiencing a particularly good shooting night, and utilizing players who are excellent spot shooters. The defense must change their coverage principles and consequently weaken the basic zone alignment. Good shooters will pay great dividends with the overload along with creating good weakside action counteracting defensive overplays.

PENETRATING THE DEFENSE

All offensive zone patterns must incorporate player movement involving penetration principles. Every team will experience an evening when everything thrown up at the basket seems to go in. Conversely, all teams will face an evening when nothing seems to go in. It is then when penetration becomes most important. The ability to penetrate may well make the difference between winning and losing. Penetrating the front line pressure of a zone can take three avenues. The ball can penetrate the zone by sharp, accurate passing inside. Second, a player can penetrate the zone by splitting the defense on a dribble. And third, penetration can be achieved by sending a cutter through the zone to the basket. Every zone offense must

Advantages and Principles of the Multiple Set Zone Offense   19

incorporate these three techniques of penetration to remain competitive and successful.

SPREADING THE DEFENSE

This offensive concept is designed to weaken the defensive pressure. Utilizing total player involvement on offense prevents the defense from overplaying, double teaming, and anticipating the next player movement or pass. Spreading the defense using the passing route will create openings for penetration. It is an excellent method to determine exactly how long the defense is willing to work. The passing option of each set will provide the necessary ball movement to accomplish the objective of spreading the defense to further enhance the opportunity to secure good percentage shots.

PASSING AND MOVING

The concept of passing and moving can be often vague in its interpretation. Passing the ball and moving for the sake of running around is simply wasting energy on offense. Ideally, the proper perspective is to work hard on defense and catch a breather on offense. Once movement is initiated it must present a scoring possibility. Four ways to pass and move effectively are:

1. Pass and move to initiate the continuity of the offensive set.
2. Pass and rotate to fill in positions for return passes and shot opportunities as dictated by the offensive pattern.
3. Pass the ball and slide behind the defense on an overplay looking for a return pass.
4. Pass and move to overload a defensive player or area and thereby force the defender to make a commitment on defensive coverage.

Used properly the passing and moving maneuvers can force the defense out of position, create player mismatches, and force the defense back towards the basket.

DEVELOPING VARIATION IN THE OFFENSIVE ATTACK

Variation and flexibility are important concepts in organizing a consistent and effective offense. Teams will prepare excellent defensive principles based on the specific offensive pattern or formation that they will face. Generally, this will have a tendency to frustrate the offense because of the specific nature of the defense employed. Being able to employ variation in either the points of penetration or the different "look" of the offense will oftentimes upset the opponent and disrupt the defense. An example will help clarify this. Team A uses a 2-1-2 zone offense. Team B generally uses a 2-3 zone defense. B by moving the middle defender up to the foul line creates almost a match-up defense which will stall the offensive attack because of the 1 to 1 basis employed. However, team A can adjust by moving the high post to a low post in forming a 2-2-1 set, or rotating to form a 1-3-1 set for example. This creates additional problems for the defense in the form of new adjustments that are needed. Consequently an offensive advantage can be gained, particularly if the defense has not been schooled to react properly to these sets. This is a major advantage of employing a multiple set zone offense.

DISRUPTING DEFENSIVE PLANS

In the majority of cases, teams prepare for upcoming opponents through the use of scouting reports. Many times a team will scout the opponent against a team employing a similar defense as their own. Consequently a team can then spend a great deal of time defensing the particular offensive maneuvers they will see and correlate this with their basic defensive alignment and adjustments. Therefore in many cases the defense can anticipate the offensive team's next movement. What a surprise when the offensive team changes its zone set and attacks from different angles and with a different "look." Example: Team A scouts B playing a 2-1-2 set against a team employing a 1-3-1 zone similar to their own. This has A making defensive adjustments to counteract and thwart the 2-1-2 movement. On game night, B comes out and sets up in a 2-2-1 set to confuse the original defensive plans and gains an offensive advantage immediately.

UTILIZING INDIVIDUAL STRENGTHS

The multiple set zone concept allows for individuality and specificity of individual strengths. After analyzing each individ-

Advantages and Principles of the Multiple Set Zone Offense 21

ual, the team can be strengthened by proper placing of personnel. Which players shoot better from one particular side of the floor? Which players have ability and quickness to drive the baseline effectively? Which players have the ability to handle the ball in traffic, in particular the high post area? Which players move better to the right or left for the shot? Which players are better offensive rebounders? These are some of the questions that can be answered by utilizing the players properly in the multiple set formations.

FORCING A DEFENSIVE COMMITMENT

Teams employing a zone defense become more secure and confident when their defensive reaction is stereotyped against a specific movement pattern in the opponent's offense. This occurs when a team employs a single offensive set and is well scouted. Defensively players respond more aggressively when they are sure if they make a mistake a teammate is willing and able to cover up. But take the same defender and isolate him on a side in a one to one ratio with an offensive player, his movement becomes hesitant and he is reluctant to gamble. This same effect will be developed by employing different sets to throw the defense off guard. In actuality the defense will be forced to commit themselves in a different situation in an unfamiliar way. Consequently defensive cohesion and effectiveness can be weakened.

CHAPTER TWO

Developing Offensive Pressures with the Multiple Set Zone Offense

The increase in the use of and sophistication of zone defenses has necessitated the movement towards a multiple zet zone offense. Some coaches feel one pattern is capable of defeating all zone defenses. However, this generally becomes the case only when a team out-personnels the opponent, in which case the pattern would prove successful because of the over-powering ability of the team.

Due to the increasing complexity of zone defenses, it is essential to create offensive variations. I find it strange that whenever defensive theory is discussed the point always revolves around the topic of types of pressure applied. This includes trapping, double teaming, jump switching, forcing the weak hand, forcing players out of position, forcing the dribble, and guiding the offensive player. But when zone offensive theory is discussed, reasons for success or failure are based on shooting performances, superior or inferior size, great or lack of second efforts, ability to penetrate, and good or poor pattern execution. Seldom if ever is the area of offensive pressure included. This

24 Developing Offensive Pressures with the Multiple Set Zone Offense

concept becomes instrumental in the multiple set zone offense. Defense becomes a lot tougher to play when forced to adjust to offensive pressure as opposed to dictating the type of pressure desired to be placed on the offense.

The types of offensive pressure created by the multiple set include creating a mismatch in personnel, forming passing triangles to create 3 on 2 situations, splitting the defense to force a commitment, weakside action to catch the defense napping or relaxing, screening the zone defenders, committing defenders out of position, penetrating with the dribble, overloading an area or player to create 2 on 1 or 1 on 0 situations for a clear shot, and the inherent pressure developed by pattern execution.

CREATING A MISMATCH

There are two methods that can be used in creating a mismatch. The first method involves mismatching players. Examples would be rotating the post men in the 2-1-2 set, exchanging the high and low post in the 1-3-1 set, and placing the tallest guard in the even front sets against the shortest defender. The objective in these maneuvers is to outsize the opponent by position. This enables the offensive player a greater opportunity to secure shots without fear of having them blocked. An important note is that player mismatches greatly decrease the number of forced and off balance shots taken.

The second method concerns mismatching a defensive area. This can be accomplished by overloading an area or side. It can be a stationary·overload as in the 1-3-1 overload set or a moving overload developed by sending players through the defense on a cutting maneuver. Overloading pressures the defense to make a decision on reacting to the ball or to the player. Indecision or wrong decisions will create scoring opportunities for the offense.

UTILIZING PASSING TRIANGLES

In forming passing triangles the objective is to create a situation where three offensive players are operating against two defensive players. This is developed by counteracting the zone defense with the proper set to take advantage of the weakness of each zone, the eventual result being a good percentage

Developing Offensive Pressures with the Multiple Set Zone Offense 25

scoring opportunity. This may be in the form of a clear jump shot, a dribble penetration for a jump shot or pass-off inside, or a drive and dropping a pass-off as the backline defenders close to stop the penetration. The passing triangles in the various sets are determined by the placement of the defensive players as dictated by their specific zone defense. Diagram 2-1 illustrates the passing triangles formed in the 2-2-1 set. These include opportunities existing between players 1-3-5 and players 2-4-5. The 2-2-1 set is effective against odd front zone defenses. Diagram 2-2 shows the passing triangles developed in the 2-1-2 set. These include players 1-2-3, 1-3-4, and 2-3-5. Likewise the 2-1-2 set is

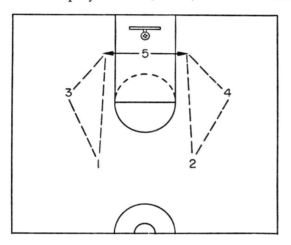

Diagram 2-1

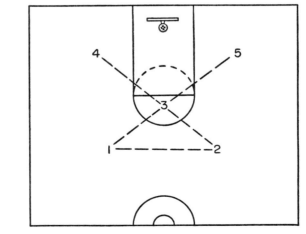

Diagram 2-2

effective against odd front zones. Diagram 2-3 shows the passing triangles in operation when employing the 1-3-1 overload set. Depending on the strongside designation, two major triangles are formed to produce possible scoring opportunities. These include players 1-2-3 and 2-3-5 when strongside left, and players 1-3-4 and 3-4-5 when strongside right. Diagram 2-4 illustrates the triangles available when operating from the standard 1-3-1 set. These include players 1-2-3, 1-3-4, 2-3-5, and 3-4-5. The 1-3-1 set is effective against even front zone defenses.

The only set unable to utilize effectively the concept of passing triangles is the 3-2 set. This is difficult because the players are too far spread to present any serious problems to the defense along these lines. The importance of the 3-2 set in future development will be discussed in later chapters.

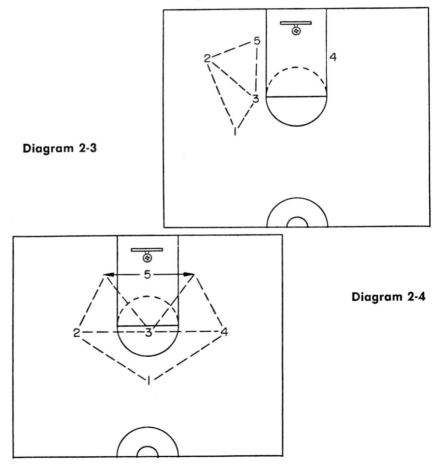

Diagram 2-3

Diagram 2-4

Developing Offensive Pressures with the Multiple Set Zone Offense 27

SPLITTING THE DEFENSE

Splitting the defense with the appropriate set forces the zone defenders to make a decision on coverage responsibility. Each set is utilized to counteract the defensive alignment and space offensive players in the gaps between defenders. This includes:

1. Utilizing the 2-2-1 set, and 2-1-2 set against a 3-2 zone.
2. Utilizing the 2-2-1 set, 2-1-2 set and 1-3-1 overload set against a 1-2-2 zone.
3. Utilizing the 1-3-1 set, 1-3-1 overload set, and 3-2 set against a 2-1-2 zone or 2-3 zone.
4. Utilizing the 2-2-1 set, and 2-1-2 set against a 1-3-1 zone.
5. Utilizing the 1-3-1 set, 1-3-1 overload set and 3-2 set against a 2-2-1 zone.

The objective of this system is to outmaneuver zone defenses by employing the proper sets designated above. By doing this, each defensive player is forced to make one of three decisions when he is gapped on either side or spaced in between by an offensive player. He can react to the ball which opens the second man for a return pass and shot. He can anticipate the return pass and the other offensive player fakes and shoots or penetrates. The third option is to gap the two offensive players which allows either player with the ball an excellent opportunity to penetrate for a good percentage shot. An illustration of this concept would be utilizing the 1-3-1 set against a 2-3 zone. Diagram 2-5 shows the possibilities that exist in gapping or spacing defensive players. These include player 1 gapping defenders A and B, 2 splitting A and D, 4 penetrating between defenders B and E. Alternative movement consists of offensive players 1 and 2 committing defender A, 1 and 4 forcing B, 1 and 3 operating against C, 2 and 5 against D, and 4 and 5 on E. All of these ideas can be applied to each set when opposing specific zone defenses for which they were designed.

EMPLOYING WEAKSIDE ACTION

The weakside of an offensive pattern is the side of the floor away from the ball or the side of the floor which has the least concentration of players. The sets which employ the weakside

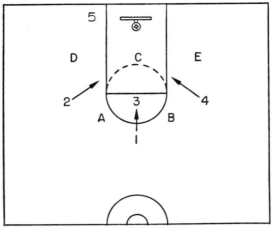

Diagram 2-5

action are the 1-3-1 set, 1-3-1 overload set, and the 2-2-1 set. There are three maneuvers used effectively from the weakside. The first action consists of the weakside player forcing the defense to relax and ignore him. This is accomplished by having him focus his attention on the ball. The weakside player must appear to be unconcerned about the movement of the ball and be patient for his opening. The ball is quickly reversed from the strongside to point to weakside for a jump shot or an opportunity to work 1 on 1 if the defense recovers slowly. This will generally occur when using the 1-3-1 overload set. The weakside player hesitates and sets his defender up as the ball moves back to the point. Diagram 2-6 illustrates defensive coverage by the 2-1-2 zone on the overload and resultant weakside action as the defense overshifts to the strongside.

The second action consists of the weakside player sliding behind the zone for a pinpoint pass and shot. The 2-2-1 set is very

Diagram 2-6

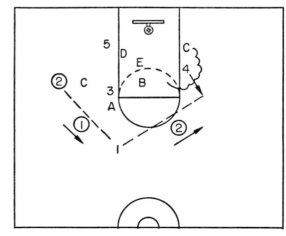

Developing Offensive Pressures with the Multiple Set Zone Offense 29

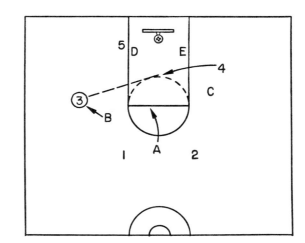

Diagram 2-7

effective in using this maneuver. Diagram 2-7 shows the operation of the 2-2-1 set against a 3-2 zone. As the ball is occupied on the strongside, the weakside player 4 initiates movement by sliding behind the defender C assigned to his area. The defender being concerned with the ball will momentarily forget the weakside player to make this maneuver possible.

The third action involves the weakside man moving to good offensive rebounding position to pick up baskets on the second or third effort. The 1-3-1 overload set utilizes this maneuver best because the defense must overshift to compensate for the strongside. The weakside player moves to an inside position on the lane anticipating a shot from the strongside. The weakside player also serves as a safety valve when the defense overplays and pressures the point, preventing a pass into the strongside wing.

SCREENING THE ZONE

Screening the zone is a very effective technique when used properly. Each defender keys on the ball but is still responsible for an offensive player in his area. This then creates a one to one ratio. By sending a cutter through the zone after passing, he can use another teammate as a screen continuing out to the corner. The ball is reversed around the perimeter of the zone to the cutter in the corner for a baseline jump shot. The 3-2 set uses this maneuver very well. Diagram 2-8 illustrates the

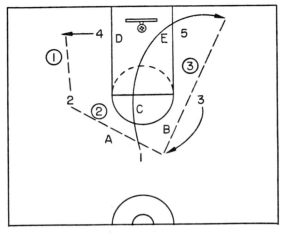

Diagram 2-8

screening possibility by sending the point (1) through the middle of the lane on his cut and clears to the opposite corner. The ball reverses around the perimeter to 1 in the corner who has used 5 to screen the zone defender in that area which would be E in this case. The momentary delay of the defensive player to react to the temporary screen will create a good percentage shot.

COMMITTING THE DEFENSE

The importance of ball movement and player action becomes apparent when discussing the concept of committing the defense. This is utilized fully in employing all the basic sets which make up the multiple set zone offense. The offensive theory is based on selecting the appropriate set to counter the zone defense and space the players to create openings. There are four ways to commit the defense. The first is gapping two defenders, which forces one of them to commit for coverage. The resulting passing action will be in the direction the defender came from because he will not be able to recover and protect against a shot. Second, a three or two situation is formed by using the concept of the passing triangle to free an offensive player for a shot. Third, the spacing of two offensive players on either side of a defender creates a situation based on the same principles of gapping and forming passing triangles. The fourth method consists of overloading, which also creates an uneven player situation favoring the offense.

Developing Offensive Pressures with the Multiple Set Zone Offense 31

PENETRATING ON A DRIBBLE

The concept of dribbling against a zone defense is a topic of controversy. Some coaches feel it disrupts the continuity of the pattern, is ineffective, and allows the defense to create additional pressure on the ball. Although these facts are basically true, dribbling when used at the right time and right place can be extremely effective. Against a zone it must be a penetrating dribble to be worthwhile.

All zone defenses can be viewed in terms of three categories. A zone can be designed to pressure the ball aggressively. A zone can be used to play strong position on the ball protecting the basket. Or a zone can sag and close off the middle lane area. Against an aggressive zone, the dribble penetration is a good offensive maneuver. The pressure or aggressive tactics will be characterized by quick movement, jumping at the ball, flooding an area, and gambling for the interception or steal. The counter movement is for the offensive player to fake first before passing. Should the defensive player anticipate the type and direction of the pass, the preliminary fake will pull him out of position. Immediately the offensive player moves on a dribble towards the basket to penetrate the front line pressure. Oftentimes he can move to the area vacated by the defender being pulled out of position. The movement is to drive all the way, pull up for a jump shot, or draw the backline defense up and pass off.

The nature of the multiple set zone offense is to counteract the zone defense by utilizing the proper sets to create various forms of offensive pressure. Accordingly, the most advantageous points to accomplish an effective dribble penetration vary with the type of zone defense employed. Even front zones are attacked by the odd front sets (1-3-1, 3-2, 1-3-1 overload) and are susceptible to penetration from the top of the key and from the wing positions at the foul line extended. Diagram 2-9 illustrates this principle employing the 1-3-1 set against a 2-1-2 zone. The possibilities of penetrating on the dribble involve player 1 between defenders A and B, 2 between defenders A and D, and 4 between defenders B and E. If the forwards react up to stop

32 *Developing Offensive Pressures with the Multiple Set Zone Offense*

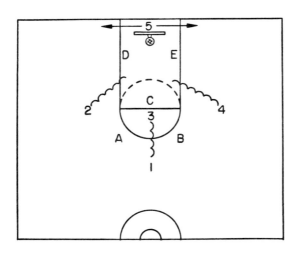

Diagram 2-9

the penetration, 5 slides to the basket along the baseline looking for a pass.

Odd front zones are attacked by the even front sets (2-2-1, 2-1-2) and in certain situations by the 1-3-1 overload. They are susceptible to penetration along the baseline, and from a 70 degree angle between the defensive point and wing man. Diagram 2-10 shows the movement possible employing the 2-2-1 set against a 1-3-1 zone. Player 1 moving between defenders A and B, 2 splitting A and D, and 5 between defenders B and E.

Dribbling is habit forming. Therefore, it must be re-emphasized that dribbling should only be used in the above fashion or as a last resort to relieve defensive pressure.

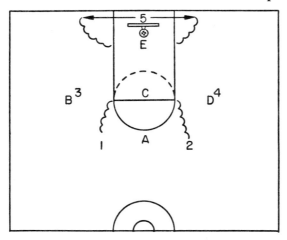

Diagram 2-10

OVERLOADING A SIDE

Overloading a side is another method of applying offensive pressure. It can be a stationary overload as employed in the 1-3-1 overload set, or a moving overload created by sending players through in a cutting or rolling maneuver. Basically the concept involves placing more offensive than there are defensive players in an area to create better scoring possibilities. The speciality of spot shooting is a premium skill to take advantage of in an overload situation. The one great advantage of overloading the offense is to force the zone defensive players out of positions normally assumed. This necessitates adjustments which may or may not prove effective. The zone then becomes more concerned about player involvement, which causes less pressure and concentration on the ball. Consequently the offense gains an advantage by applying pressure to the defense.

EMPHASIZING PATTERN EXECUTION

Pattern execution implies properly utilizing an offensive pattern to gain full effectiveness through player movement. It involves the right movement at the right time in the right place. Pattern execution is based on the four ingredients of player ability, player confidence, pattern feasibility, and precision movement. Player ability is a determining factor in the type of offensive pattern employed as well as the proper placing of personnel to take advantage of special abilities. In high school this element is extremely important based on the simple fact that each season must be approached differently because of different levels of talent and abilities that are available. Recruiting of course cannot be considered to select players for a particular system of play. Consequently the system must be adjusted to the personnel available. Without contradicting the above statement, the multiple set can be used every year with minor adjustments. The difference is proper positioning of players as well as emphasizing particular sets or options based on the ability level.

The second element under consideration is player confidence in the selected system. Confidence is instilled by achieving a measure of success developed through its use along with the

34 Developing Offensive Pressures with the Multiple Set Zone Offense

player's interest and desire to run it. This last comment may seem strange, but as coaches we will have to swallow our pride at times. A highly intricate system will be effective, but if players are not completely sold on it or are unable to fully understand it doubts will arise. It then becomes better to eliminate the complex nature and incorporate something more basic and easier to understand. The game is for the players. They must enjoy it and gain a certain amount of satisfaction to consider it a success. Confidence is a direct result of success.

The third factor necessary for improving pattern execution revolves around the feasibility of the pattern. All offensive patterns employ special abilities in specific positions to operate effectively and successfully. If the players available do not fit the specifications of the offensive system, it is unlikely that any degree of success will be achieved.

The final element under consideration in pattern execution is precision movement of the players. All players must know exactly what to do and perform exactly as the offensive pattern dictates to be effective. How often does a cutter moving through the defense jog through the middle without looking for a return pass? Or how often do the players not involved in the key action of the option perform their task haphazardly? All players must be instructed to execute their movement quickly, efficiently, and with good timing. Players must be taught to realize that although they may not be directly involved in the scoring attempt, their ability to execute properly will open up opportunities for other players.

In concluding this topic, offensive pressure can be formed in a variety of ways. The coach will determine the most effective methods to be used based on personnel appraisal. Players must be alerted to all the possibilities that exist and instructed to react automatically in many situations that develop. All forms of offensive pressure will not be effective against all teams. Scouting reports, repetition in practice, trial and error, and actual game experimentation are the ways to determine which forms of offensive pressure are best designed for each team.

CHAPTER THREE

The Basic Positions in the Multiple Set Zone Offense

A factor for success of any offensive system is the proper placing of personnel. Each position possesses certain characteristics and has a unique role which when executed properly will create effective offensive movement. The coach is responsible for selecting and placing players in the positions where their individual abilities will be an asset to the team. There have been many instances where players have been played out of position and both the individual and the team have suffered. One glaring example of this comes to mind in one of our past experiences. A former player for us made a transition from a second line guard to an all league forward in one year. "Mike" played guard for three years in primarily a reserve capacity. He was 6'2" and possessed a good jump shot but lacked confidence to operate efficiently at a guard position to take advantage of his size and shooting ability. By a stroke of fate and not coaching strategy we were able to exploit him in a forward position. It occured in the sectional playoffs at the end of his junior year. He had played as a guard during the season, but injuries to our first and second team

35

centers forced some drastic changes for the playoffs. We inserted Mike as a forward and he responded with 16 points and 10 rebounds. Although 6'2" is short for a forward, Mike made up for his lack of size with excellent maneuverability in the lane area, a quick first step on his drive, the knack of sensing where the rebound was going, and the ability to penetrate along the baseline to the basket. The success of his transition from guard to forward in his senior year is apparent by both individual statistics and the overall team record. Our record was 16-2 and his individual statistics included: 18.3 points per game average for 21 minutes per game playing time, 72.5% from the foul line, 48% from the field, third in team rebounding, and third in team assists.

Each year with the changeover of material it is necessary to analyze and evaluate the ability of each player in the most effective way to benefit the team.

PLAYER ANALYSIS

There are questions to be answered in determining a player's best position, primary, and secondary responsibilities.

1. *Does the player follow his shot effectively?*

   A basic concept in offensive basketball is to teach players to follow their shots. They will have the best idea where the ball will most likely rebound to. However, every player will not always follow his shot and many times a player will effect his accuracy by not doing it well. Severe criticism on the part of the coach will only hinder his effort. This same player who fails to follow his shot effectively may be outstanding in the area of recovering quickly on defense to prevent a fast break. His primary responsibility should then be to maintain team balance and react quickly from offense to defense.

2. *Is the player primarily a spot shooter?*

   This is essential in developing an outside scoring attack against zone defenses. Pre-season shooting records can prove invaluable in this area. A minor adjustment only in positioning is necessary. The result is utilizing a player in

The Basic Positions in the Multiple Set Zone Offense   *37*

a position where he has more confidence and feels most comfortable in. Some players will shoot much better from one side of the court than the other. Therefore, changing the wing positions, guard positions, or low post positions may result in better shooting percentages. In the multiple set system this phase is extremely important. It is based on counteracting each zone defense with a specific set designed to take advantage of specialized shooting abilities.

3. *Does a player move to good offensive rebounding position effectively?*

This knowledge is extremely important. A player regardless of size often possesses the savvy and ability to pick up "garbage" baskets on stray rebounds and occasional three point plays. He can also be valuable in tieing up the defensive rebounder to prevent an outlet pass initiating a fast break opportunity. In many cases it would be wise to keep this type of player as close to the basket as possible.

4. *Is the player primarily a scorer or feeder?*

It isn't often when the average high school basketball team possesses more than one outstanding shooter or ball handler. Consequently it is important that the coach carefully analyze each individual player and his best attributes to decide on his future role to the team and the responsibility he is expected to assume.

5. *Is the player mobile in the lane area?*

Many field goal opportunities and baskets have been eliminated against zone defenses because of three-second violations, bobbled attempts, and poor pass receptions. It becomes imperative to recognize players who are quick and able to handle the ball in traffic. There are not many boys who possess the ability to be a scoring threat in the lane area.

6. *Does the player make a good transition from offense to defense?*

Many cheap baskets are given up due to failure of the

players to react quickly from offense to defense. Statistics are an excellent method to determine whether or not a player is contributing more or allowing more points to the opponent. A player who makes the transition consistently and effectively is a tremendous asset to any team. His value is measured by the number of fast break baskets he eliminates through his efforts.

7. *Does the player execute the offensive pattern properly?*

Basketball is a game of teamwork and necessitates the unity of all five players on the floor to achieve success. The common bond to achieve team unity is an offensive pattern executed properly with the team ideal in mind. Particularly against zone defenses there is no place for one on one concentration, free play, or individual heroics.

8. *Does the player possess a "take charge" attitude?*

Every high school basketball team regardless of player ability will endure both a streak and slump period. It is a tremendous plus factor to have a player when things are going bad to have the ability to take charge, settle the team down, and regroup a total effort. Sometimes this ability lies in the seventh, eighth, and ninth men on the squad. An important attribute such as this must be discovered as soon as possible. This is accomplished by talking to previous coaches, observing the players daily in practice sessions, and playing everybody equally in pre-season scrimmages to discover this talent. A player possessing this attribute is worth his weight in gold.

9. *Does each player understand his responsibility and realize his obligation to the team?*

Many situations arise in games which require precision reaction on the part of every team member. Among these are included jump ball situations, out-of-bounds plays, last second shot patterns, semi-stall patterns, and all offensive patterns designed to take advantage of individual abilities. These require complete concentration and execution on the part of all team members. Every player must place the team concept ahead of individual success. Any

The Basic Positions in the Multiple Set Zone Offense 39

player not willing to sacrifice for the benefit of the team must be re-evaluated in terms of his overall contribution to the team.

10. *Does the player react well under pressure?*

Players possess a great variety of abilities and unique personalities. There are three types of players that can be distinguished. The first category consists of players who perform well in both practice sessions and games. These are the most consistent players on the squad and definitely will be the major reason for the overall success of the team. The second category of players is those that perform well in practice but poorly in games. Their problem is primarily lack of confidence. It is a good point to play these players early in the game to give them experience and a chance to build confidence without a lot of pressure which might be present in the latter stages of a game. They will be a valuable asset if allowed the opportunity to contribute to the team. Sometimes this type of player is forgotten or benched because of a mistake made in an early season game under pressure. The third category of players is those who perform poorly in practice but more than adequate in games. This situation may cause a problem in team morale if not understood properly. It may be caused by a poor attitude, lack of motivation, or the ability to perform best in front of spectators. Whatever the reason, it must be diagnosed to keep harmony on the team. This group of players likewise can be an asset to the team if the answer can be solved. It is imperative to discover the players who will react well to pressure situations. There are even some players who thrive on pressure. Examination in this area is critical and a major reason for the team success or failure. Oftentimes checking with the junior varsity or ninth grade coach will reveal the boys that are capable of performing under pressure.

PLAYER POSITIONS

The *Point Position* is formed at the top of the key area one to two steps off depending on defensive pressure. The point position initiates the offense and is instrumental in the 1-3-1 set, 3-2 set, and the 1-3-1 overload set. Diagram 3-1 shows the relative position of the point player.

The player selected for the point position should possess the following characteristics:

1. Handle the ball extremely well and possess a variety of passes to penetrate the defense.
2. Possess ability to dribble equally well with either hand.
3. Be a scoring threat from 15-18' particularly from the key area.
4. Possess quickness to recover rapidly on defense.
5. Possess mental alertness to analyze the defense and react accordingly.
6. Be unselfish in his attitude because at times his overall performance will not be recognized with the point getters.

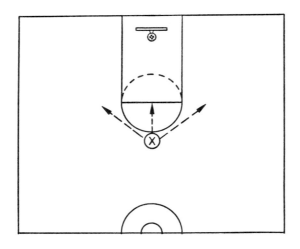

Diagram 3-1

The responsibilities assigned to this position include:

1. Instituting the offensive pattern.
2. Initiating the correct offensive option.
3. Working two-man passing situations with the wingmen (1-3-1 and overload).
4. Incorporating triangle passing situations with the wingmen and high post (1-3-1 and overload).

The Basic Positions in the Multiple Set Zone Offense 41

5. Shooting a good percentage from the key area to keep the defense honest.
6. Adjusting to changing defenses and alerting the rest of the team to run the proper set and option.
7. Exhibiting patience and poise to set the offense up and work for the good shot.
8. Concentrating on attacking the weak areas of the defense.
9. Maintaining floor balance on the shot to prevent a fast break from starting.
10. Relaying information from the bench to the rest of the team.

The *High Post position* is established along the foul line and is utilized in the 1-3-1 set, 2-1-2 set, and 1-3-1 overload set. Diagram 3-2 shows the area responsible for the high post player.

Diagram 3-2

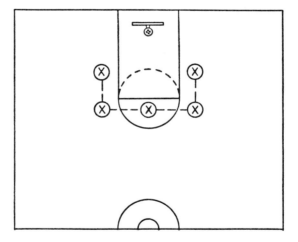

The player selected for this position must possess the following characteristics to be effective.

1. Agile and mobile to be a constant scoring threat.
2. Quick to move from side high to middle high to side high along the foul line as the ball is passed around the perimeter.
3. Able to score with a turn around shot from 15'.

4. Able to reverse and drive left or right depending on the situation.
5. Aggressive and be able to get to the basket for offensive rebounding possibilities.

The offensive responsibilities for this position include:
1. Receiving a pass and pivoting for a shot or pass off underneath.
2. Feeding off to the wingmen as the defense sags on the ball.
3. Being a primary offensive rebounder.
4. Quickness to maneuver to an open shot on the roll options.
5. Being a relief valve for players being trapped in corners or on the sideline.
6. Being the primary consideration in the offensive flow through the middle.

The *Low Post position* is established in the area along the foul line opposite the basket on either the left or right side. The single low post is active in the 1-3-1 set, overload set, and 2-2-1 set. Diagram 3-3 shows the area responsibilities of the single low post player.

The single low post position is occupied by a player with the following characteristics:

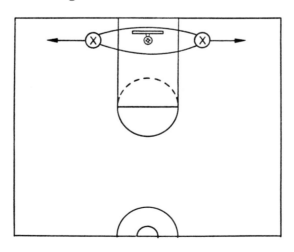

Diagram 3-3

The Basic Positions in the Multiple Set Zone Offesne 43

1. Generally the best offensive rebounder on the team.
2. Usually the biggest player on the team.
3. Mobile enough to patrol the baseline effectively and efficiently.
4. Possess a fair hook shot as an added scoring move.
5. Able to receive the ball and pass it quickly and accurately.
6. Able to hit a jump shot consistently from 8-12'.

The player selected for this position assumes the following responsibilities:

1. Clearing himself along the baseline for a shot.
2. Handling the ball well enough to assume the role of feeder for cutters moving through the middle.
3. Mobile enough to gain good offensive rebounding position for the tip in and possible three-point play.
4. Capable of being a scoring threat with a corner jump shot to keep the defense honest and in the process draw them away from the basket.
5. Dribbling and driving adequately to penetrate along the baseline when the defense commits itself.
6. Moving freely from corner to corner as part of the low post requirements.
7. Faking well to free himself to receive penetration passes.
8. Responsibility in defensive rebounding to delay the outlet pass preventing a fast break from starting.

The *Wing Position* originates at a 45 degree angle from the basket at the foul line extended approximately mid-distance to the sideline. This allows the wing players greater area and maneuverability to operate with the ball. The wing position comes into play in the 1-3-1 set, 2-2-1 set, 3-2 set, and the overload set. A slight modification exists for the strongside and weakside wing positions in the overload. The strongside wing splits the low and high post midway and also half the distance to the sideline. The weakside wing establishes his position likewise splitting the high and low post, but stationed tight on the foul lane. Diagram 3-4 shows the normal positioning for a wingman.

44   *The Basic Positions in the Multiple Set Zone Offense*

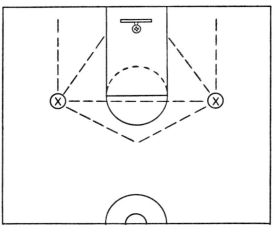

Diagram 3-4

The wing positions will usually generate 80-90% of the outside scoring punch when in effect. The characteristics desirable for this position are:

1. Best jump shooters on the team.
2. Dribble both ways equally well to prevent the defense from overplaying.
3. Quick enough to react to rebounding position or maintain defensive balance depending on the situation.
4. Mentally alert because they are instrumental in all three options of each set.
5. Mobile enough to get to the basket quickly for offensive rebounding position.

The responsibilities of the players in this position are:

1. Taking the majority of outside scoring attempts.
2. Determining which option will be run upon reception of pass.
3. Primary cutting action in sets employing a high post.
4. Penetrating the front line defense.
5. Forming two-man passing situations with the point, high post, and low post in the odd front sets and guard, high post, and low post in the even front sets.
6. Forming passing triangles with the point-high post, point-low post, and high post-low post.
7. Providing relief for corner pressure on the low post.

The Basic Positions in the Multiple Set Zone Offense 45

The *Double Guard* positions are assumed 1-2 steps outside the top of the key about fifteen feet apart. The double guard situation comes into play in the even front sets (2-2-1, 2-1-2). The players selected for the guard positions must possess the same characteristics previously outlined as those assumed by the point position.

The *Double Low Post* players take a basic position even with the basket and one step off the foul lane. The double low post positions are established in the 3-2 set, and 2-1-2 sets. The responsibilities and characteristics for this position have already been outlined in the coverage of the single low post position.

CHAPTER FOUR

Developing an Interior Attack
with the Multiple Set
Zone Offense

There are two basic methods of attacking zone defenses to provide a scoring thrust. The first method involves the perimeter attack, which is accomplished by the passing option of each offensive set. It consists of moving the ball quickly and accurately around the outside of the zone looking for openings. The success naturally is dependent upon the ability of the players to convert the 15-18' jump shots. It is also necessary to split the defense and penetrate to secure closer shots. This can be a very effective method particularly for teams possessing outstanding shooters. However, it can also be disastrous when the shots are not dropping. This problem seems to occur more often when the zone offense is based entirely on this concept of outside shooting. To complement this form of attack and create more offensive pressure, it is necessary to incorporate an interior attack. The effectiveness of the interior attack is built around the cut and roll options of each set. This can be much more consistent than relying solely on

48 *Developing an Interior Attack with the Multiple Set Zone Offense*

outside shooting. It is also the best way to demoralize a zone defense by securing the short 8-10' jumpers, short hook shots, layups, and occasional three-point plays. Zone offensive consistency revolves around the initiation of both forms of attack complementing each other. The ingredients necessary are teamwork, execution, timing, and good communication.

THE HIGH POST OPTIONS

The high post is an essential position to develop a scoring threat in the lane area. There are six scoring maneuvers to be developed from the high post area. A player in this position must practice daily and become proficient in each.

1. Receive a pass from the point or guard position and roll right or left for a drive, hook shot, or pull up for a jump shot.
2. Roll right or left to a semi-low post and receive a pass from the wing or low post man wide in the corner for a jump shot, hook shot, or power move to the basket.
3. Receive a pass from the point, guard or wing and turn left or right for a 15' jump shot from the foul line.

In the normal offensive play in the multiple set zone offense the high post operative will receive a possible pass from one of four basic positions. These are the point, guard, wing, and low post moving to a wide position in the corner. The first consideration is to select the personnel that will occupy the high post position. This will be dependent on the individual coaches' evaluation of the best player suited for the high post position. Body build, coordination, agility, and shooting accuracy are primary factors to consider when selecting a player for this position.

A player does not automatically become a skilled operative from this position simply because he is selected to play it. After the initial selection has been made, the player must be exposed to the possibilities that will be presented throughout a game to acquaint him with the necessary reactions needed to become a scoring threat. The first stage of development involves familiarizing the player with the three basic positions of the high post area. These are middle foul line, side high right, and side high left. Diagram 4-1 shows the three positions that will be assumed by the high post player.

Developing an Interior Attack with the Multiple Set Zone Offense 49

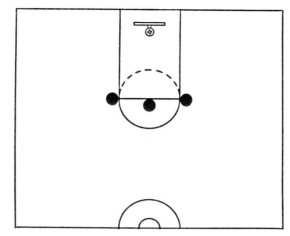

Diagram 4-1

The coach or a manager in the initial stage of learning will proceed to feed the high post in the three positions from the normal point position. This occurs during the practice allotment for individual skill improvement. This is a valuable time for the coach to instruct, make corrections, and convey additional information for improving performance in the position. The six scoring actions described earlier will be performed from each of the positions upon reception of the pass. No defensive action will be involved as the player is gaining initial confidence in his movement and becoming accustomed to the position. As the player gets acquainted with the various maneuvers, the second stage of learning begins. The actual player involved in running the offense from the point or guard position will continue to feed the high post for his individual maneuvers.

After timing and communication between the players improve, the next step is to introduce a defensive player on the high post player. Again confidence is extremely important in mastering the proper techniques. Therefore, a defensive player shorter than the high post is utilized to accord more success in securing shots. Three defensive techniques are used to defend the high post. The first position is directly behind to prevent a drive but allowing the high post to receive an uncontested pass. The second position is defending the high post on the side of the ball with an arm in front to discourage and deflect passes inside. This teaches the high post to use his body in shielding the defense to receive a pass. The third technique involves the defender play-

50 *Developing an Interior Attack with the Multiple Set Zone Offense*

ing in front of the high post to prevent a direct chest or bounce pass from being made. However, this is seldom used unless the point defender drops back in front of the high post to stop a direct pass in. This is when the low pass to the high post backing down the lane is introduced. All of these defensive techniques are performed to contest the high post. As a fair degree of success is achieved, a defender of equal size is introduced for the post to operate against. When the proper movement is achieved, the two, three, and four man situations which will be described in chapter nine are brought into play.

Finally the coordination of the complete unit based on timing and execution is developed. The development of a scoring threat in the high post area is not an easy task. It takes time, practice, patience and understanding. There is no set rule as to how long is spent on each stage of learning. The coach must decide when it is advisable to move on. The development of a player must be handled in a step by step fashion explained by the saying "you have to learn how to walk before you can run."

THE LOW POST OPTIONS

The low post is equally important in developing an inside scoring advantage. There are five scoring maneuvers developed from the low post position.

1. Receive a pass, fake, and drive the baseline left or right.
2. Receive a pass, fake to drive the defender back and take a 15-18' corner jumper.
3. Receive a pass, fake the baseline drive, penetrate to the lane area for a jump shot or continue across the lane for a hook shot.
4. Sliding to the basket when the high post turns with the ball drawing the attention of the backline defense.
5. Remaining tight on the lane, receive a pass and execute a turn around jump shot, hook shot, or power layup.

The low post operative will receive the ball in his position from one of three players. The wingman in the 2-2-1 set, 1-3-1 set, 3-2 set, and overload set will deliver the ball in the tight lane position or as the low post moves wide. The guard in the 2-1-2 set will deliver the pass primarily to the low post moving wide to the corner. The high post will drop a pass off to the low

Developing an Interior Attack with the Multiple Set Zone Offense 51

post sliding behind the defense into the immediate basket area. Diagram 4-2 shows the five positions the low post will find himself in to receive a possible pass. They include the right corner, left corner, tight lane right, tight lane left, and immediate basket area.

The skills to develop from both the left and right corner positions include:

1. Receiving a pass from the wing or guard position and turning to face the basket immediately without wasting a dribble.
2. Fake and take a jump shot in balance.

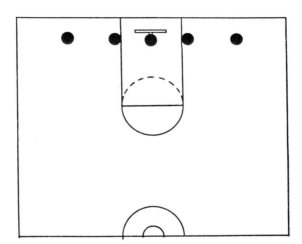

Diagram 4-2

3. Fake and drive the baseline.
4. Fake and drive the middle to pull up for a jump shot, drive to the basket, or slide across the lane for a short hook shot.
5. Pass to a cutter moving through the middle.
6. Pass to the high post rolling to the basket.

All of these skills are practiced first with no defense contesting the movement. After the timing and execution are improved, a defensive player is introduced. The defensive player is instructed to provide token resistance only to allow the proper action to continue without frustrating the offensive player. The final stage involves the defense contesting the offensive

52 *Developing an Interior Attack with the Multiple Set Zone Offense*

player head to hand in a 1 on 1 situation to sharpen the skills.

The skills to develop from the tight left lane and tight right lane position include:

1. Receiving a pass inside using the body as a shield to protect the ball.
2. Turn around jump shot towards the baseline.
3. Turn around jump shot towards the middle.
4. Hook shot leaning towards the baseline.
5. Hook shot leaning towards the middle.
6. Power layup towards the baseline.

These maneuvers likewise are learned without a defensive player. After preliminary success, a defender is introduced to provide token resistance. The final stage is to allow the defense to contest and jockey for position with the offensive player.

The skills to develop around the immediate basket area include:

1. Receiving a pass and moving across the lane for a left or right hand hook using the backboard.
2. Receiving a pass and performing a reverse layup left or right off the backboard.
3. Perform a jumping layup without a dribble after receiving a pass.
4. Receiving a pass in the air, turning and laying it in under control before returning to the floor.

This group of maneuvers is difficult to practice with a defensive player. In a game the ability of the high post to deliver a pass to an open man under the basket is an automatic response to a defender being drawn out of position. The timing must be excellent to prevent three second violations. However, time in practice is spent on the low post sliding into the lane area performing the skills outlined. A stop watch is introduced to apply some pressure as well as alerting the players to realize exactly how long they have to attempt a shot without committing a three-second violation.

These offensive possibilities that can be generated have been examined in terms of a low post operative opening up scoring attempts as a single individual. In the 3-2 set and 2-1-2 set additional opportunities can be presented with the double low post

Developing an Interior Attack with the Multiple Set Zone Offense 53

working together in exchanging, crossing, and screening for one another.

THE LOW POST-HIGH POST EXCHANGE

The low-high post exchange is an integral part of any inside scoring attack. Many times as the low post and high post positions are assumed in a stationary fashion, defenders have an opportunity to overplay or front the offensive player. Because the defense does not have to react to movement, it makes their job easier as well as making it more difficult to pass inside the zone. Therefore, it is necessary at times to create movement by having the post players exchange. The primary reasons for creating this type of movement are:

1. Force the defense to play a normal position on the offensive players.
2. Keep the defense inside the lane area busy to open penetration points for cutting teammates.
3. The defense must respond to the inside movement and cover each offensive player until another defender picks him up. When this occurs a momentary opening will exist as the defenders shift their assignments.

The best passing angle enabling a player to pass inside to a high post rolling or a low post moving high is at a forty-five degree angle, which is the wing position at the foul line extended. Therefore, the 1-3-1 set and 1-3-1 overload are the formations that make this exchange available and effective. The post exchange normally takes place when the ball moves to the weakside wing position. This allows the high post to roll to the ball and the low post to move towards the ball when the high post clears. Diagram 4-3 shows the proper inside movement in the high-low post exchange.

Execution of the movement includes the point (1) passing to the weakside wing (4). High post (3) rolls toward the ball and down the lane to a low post position. The low post (5) delays until 3 is no longer a scoring threat and proceeds to break to an open spot in the lane. If he does not receive an immediate pass, he continues up to the high post position on the foul line. 4 has the option to pass to 3 moving wide to a corner position initiating a cut maneuver or pass back to the point. The point

54 *Developing an Interior Attack with the Multiple Set Zone Offense*

can pass to 2 who has now become the weakside wing and the high-low exchange can operate again without any break in the continuity of the pattern. The most important ingredient in achieving success with the exchange is timing. Poor timing can result in the cooperating players covering each other to prevent a pass inside.

In learning the proper technique the procedure is to first use a dummy situation. This consists of exposing the players to receiving a pass on the move. This is not a small item to consider. Many players have difficulty receiving a pass in close quarters, in balance, and ready to make a scoring move with-

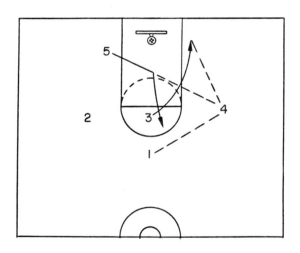

Diagram 4-3

out being guilty of a traveling violation. A great deal of time is spent on passing from the wing position to the high post rolling with no defense contesting the action. Next the pass is made to the low post moving towards the ball to an open spot in the lane without any defense involved. Both players begin moving together to get the actual feeling of the exchange. Finally, a 1-3-1 formation is established with a continuous passing action around the horn to the weakside wing initiating the exchange.

The number of times the action will occur during a game depends on the defensive alignment and coverage inside.

Developing an Interior Attack with the Multiple Set Zone Offense 55

One particular game comes to mind when considering the high-low exchange providing the impetus to win an important game. We were playing a team that specialized in a matchup defense originating from a 2-1-2 formation. We decided to operate from a 1-3-1 overload initially to take advantage of our best shooter from the strongside wing position. The defense failed to over-shift on the strongside and as the game progressed we maintained a 5-7 point lead. At the start of the fourth quarter the defense overshifted to take away the good percentage shot from the strongside wing. We started to force shots and the lead diminished until the game was tied with about four minutes to play. In a timeout we decided to run the high-low exchange exclusively to see how the defense would react. The plan was to initiate the ball with the strongside to draw the defense over. Immediately the ball was reversed around to the weakside wing. The low post defender pivoted to face the movement of the ball around the horn. Consequently he lost sight of the offensive low post in his area. As the high post cleared on his roll the high defender followed. A defensive mixup resulted because the low defender stayed low watching the ball as well as the high defender following the roll. This vacated the lane and permitted the low post an open spot to move to for a 12' jump shot. He succeeded in hitting four baskets in a row and turned a close game into a 60-47 win.

Each game is considered by itself in preparation. Any time an adjustment or minor change can make the difference between a win and a loss, we attempt to make it. If a particular maneuver is only presented once in a season and is successful, it was worth the time spent in practice perfecting it.

THE DOUBLE LOW POST EXCHANGE

The low post exchange action is another technique designed to strengthen the inside attack. This will occur in the sets employing a double low post, which are the 2-1-2 and 3-2. Three types of exchanges can take place to provide movement along the baseline. Diagram 4-4 show a simple lane exchange by the low post players.

The lane exchange is used to create a player mismatch. In certain instances we desire players to exchange to send a more mobile offensive player against a less mobile defender. Another possibility is to exchange and create a mismatch by size allowing the offensive player greater opportunity to become a scoring threat. An example explaining this would be two players 6' 5" and 6' 3" occupying the low post positions. The two low defenders are 6' 3" and 6' 2". Two matchup possibilities exist. Matching up the 6' 5" player in the zone of the 6' 2" defender allows the offensive player to overpower the area. The other alternative is to align the players in a normal size matchup to give the offensive players a height edge in both positions. The

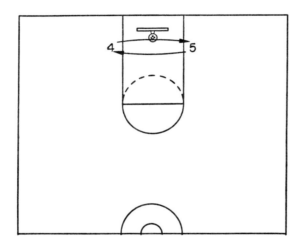

Diagram 4-4

matchup selection will be dependent on a number of factors within the game.

The second exchange action consists of a scissors maneuver with the low posts 4 and 5 moving together to create an opening. The intended receiver passes by first on the baseline using the other low post as a temporary sereen. This is used when the defense is assuming man to man principles or if the ball is to be passed to a specific low post to initiate the offensive pattern. Diagram 4-5 shows the scissors action.

The third exchange consists of one low post screening across

Developing an Interior Attack with the Multiple Set Zone Offense 57

for the other low post to receive a pass in the corner. Diagram 4-6 shows this action.

Low post (4) is being overplayed and therefore prevented from receiving a pass-in. 4 accepts the fact and remains tight on the lane. 5 proceeds to move across the lane using 4 as a screen and continuing to the corner for a pass. After 5 has cleared, 4 simply steps across the lane to the spot vacated by 5 to maintain offensive balance.

THE LOW POST LOOP

In many instances the action of the low post player is limited either by the nature of the offense or by the reaction of the backline defense to his movement. Particularly when the passing options are employed the backline defense will step up and prevent

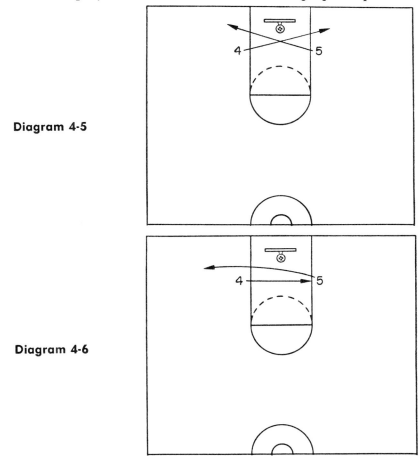

Diagram 4-5

Diagram 4-6

58   *Developing an Interior Attack with the Multiple Set Zone Offense*

the low post from receiving a pass. When this occurs it is necessary and advantageous to employ a looping maneuver by the low post. Utilizing the low post player opposite the ball to move to an open spot towards the ball from behind the defense can create additional scoring opportunities. The looping action takes place in the 2-1-2 set, 2-2-1 set, and 3-2 set. It occurs immediately following the cutting action of a player moving through the defense on his penetration. There will be a momentary lull by the defense which will allow the low post on the opposite side an opportunity to loop back towards the ball after the cutter clears. Diagram 4-7 shows the looping action as it occurs in the 3-2 set.

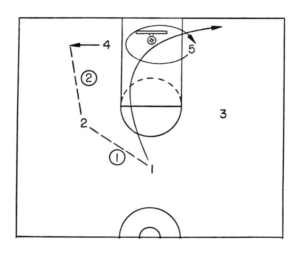

Diagram 4-7

Player 2 passes to low post 4 moving wide to the corner. 1 cuts through the middle of the lane to the basket and eventually out to the opposite corner. After 1 clears the basket area, low post 5 loops into the lane looking for a quick pass from 4 if he is open. Otherwise he continues back to his original low post position.

It is necessary to have player movement to create openings. A maneuver such as this can pay dividends if the players are made to realize the importance of quickness. Dummy practice improving the proper timing of both players involved is essential to make this maneuver practical and effective.

Developing an Interior Attack with the Multiple Set Zone Offense   59

THE LOW POST ROLL

At times the low defenders will overplay or front the low post players. In this situation a low post roll maneuver is implemented to take advantage of and produce an additional scoring opportunity inside the defense. It is used in the 2-2-1 set and 3-2 set with the absence of a high post. The movement is determined by the side of the floor the ball is brought up. In the case of the 2-2-1 set, as the ball is advanced the low post moves to the same side of the ball. When the ball is in offensive range the low post moves to a semi-high post position on the lane. The ball is passed to the wing position same side and he looks inside to deliver a pass. The defender will overplay the low post to the baseline side to deny a pass in. Immediately the ball is reversed back to the guard (2). 2 passes to the other guard (1). 1 passes into the wing position to 3. Meanwhile 5 has pivoted, putting his defender on his back out of position. As 3 receives the ball, 5 rolls across the lane to the basket and back to his original low post position. Oftentimes he will be open on this roll. Otherwise he continues out to the corner to initiate the basic offensive action of the pattern. Diagram 4-8 shows the low post roll as it occurs in the 2-2-1 set.

Diagram 4-8

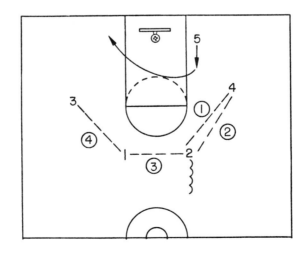

THE WEAKSIDE SIFT

The weakside sift is an offensive maneuver designed to weave back through the defense to the ball. It is totally determined by defensive positioning and freedom is accorded to the offensive player to perform this action. Whenever the perimeter passing attack is in effect, all players are expected to analyze the defense and move to an open spot for a pass when it exists. The sifting action only occurs with the players opposite the ball due to the nature of a zone defense where all players turn their attention to key on the ball. Consequently, offensive players on the opposite side of the ball are momentarily forgotten, allowing them to seek open spots by sifting through the defense from behind. This maneuver is most effective in the sets operating without a high post as it allows the weakside players more operating room in the lane.

THE LOW POST FLASH

The low post can be very effective flashing into the lane area. The low post player must time his maneuver and be quick to avoid 3-second violations. This action is most effective in the sets which do not incorporate a high post. This allows more operating room and less congestion for the low post to make his move. Therefore, the 2-2-1 set and 3-2 set make best use of this maneuver. In the 3-2 set the low post opposite the wing player with the ball attempts the flash action into the lane. In the 2-2-1 set the low post waits and momentarily delays until the wing on the opposite side has the ball before he flashes into the lane looking for a pass.

THE INSIDE ROTATION

The inside rotation action is primarily associated with the 1-3-1 overload set. The reasons for rotating the inside players include:

1. Attempting to create player mismatches in size and ability.
2. Taking advantage of offensive strengths or defensive weaknesses.
3. Forcing defensive changes in the lane area creating temporary openings for penetration.

Developing an Interior Attack with the Multiple Set Zone Offense 61

4. Testing defensive reaction to player movement.
5. Varying the offensive attack to produce additional scoring chances.

Diagram 4-9 shows the rotation of players in the 1-3-1 overload set.

The strongside wing (2) normally assumes primary responsibility with the ball. As the defense overshifts to compensate for the overload, players 3-4-5 institute the rotation. 3 moves first by sliding down the lane. 5 clears across the lane. 4 hesitates until both 3 and 5 clear the lane then times his break to an open spot. He continues across the lane and becomes the high post.

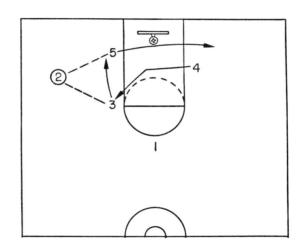

Diagram 4-9

SUMMARY

In summarizing this section on developing an inside attack against zone defenses there are important principles to use as guidelines.

1. Inside player movement to be effective must have a player moving away from the ball and a weakside player moving towards the ball or available opening.
2. Screening and exchanging by the post players keep the lane defenders busy and unable to apply undue pressure denying passes inside.

62 *Developing an Interior Attack with the Multiple Set Zone Offense*

3. Rolling movement by the high post is basic to developing an inside attack.
4. Weakside sifting to split the defense is an effective maneuver to secure shots inside the lane.
5. Looping to the basket can catch the defense relaxing on their responsibilities.
6. Flashing into the lane keeps the defense honest and prevents the defense from keying entirely on the ball.
7. Rotating players inside to new positions can create player mismatches for an offensive advantage.

All of these concepts are developed through practice. The teaching sequence involves first utilizing the player only in the movement pattern desired. Corrections are made to establish proper position and body movement. Defense is then introduced to provide token resistance only. The next stage involves the defense applying full pressure on the various actions. Two, three, and four player breakdown drills are introduced to improve learning and timing. The final stage incorporates the total team concept to improve overall timing and execution.

CHAPTER FIVE

The Offensive Patterns in
the Multiple Set Zone Offense

The multiple set zone offense was created to obtain continuous scoring possibilities against the many variations of zone defenses. A general approach of combating all zones with one basic offensive set or pattern is becoming too difficult. Unless a team is overpowering physically or clearly possesses superior talent to begin with, variations on offense are needed to provide a consistent attack.

Instituting different sets into an offensive pattern allows for greater success against all forms of zone defenses. Players gain a great deal of confidence knowing that they possess the necessary tools to operate effectively against the types of zones they will encounter. Incorporating different set formations increases flexibility on offense and takes advantage of individual specialized shooting abilities.

The concept of the multiple set zone offense is not new, but many coaches are doubtful of the ability of the players to handle the variations. Breaking down the different sets to apply basic player movement principles serves three important purposes. Understanding by the players is enhanced because of similar movement patterns developed in the same situations occurring

64   *The Offensive Patterns in the Multiple Set Zone Offense*

in the different sets. Execution is a primary aim and the similar options provide for this through repetition in practice as each set is perfected. And third, the variations in formations afford the players a change of pace coupled with a new look which oftentimes means the difference between winning and losing.

There are five formations which make up the multiple set. These include two odd front sets specifically designed to combat even front zone defenses. They are the 1-3-1 Cut and Roll Set, and the 3-2 Baseline Screen Set. There are two even front sets designed specifically to combat odd front zones. They are the 2-1-2 Perimeter Set, and the 2-2-1 Weakside Slide Set. The fifth set is designed to take advantage of outstanding shooting ability and can be used at times against all zone defenses. This is the 1-3-1 Overload Set. Together the five sets supply the necessary tools to cope with any zone defense encountered.

Each of the sets has three basic options for continuity and are similar in nature for simplicity and understanding. The first basic maneuver is the passing option. It is based on pure ball movement by the players to secure good percentage scoring opportunities. At times the basic passing of each set can be extremely effective against an over-aggressive zone. This particular option keeps the offense spread, the players in good floor balance at all times, and most important the ball moving. Individual ability is exploited with this option. Team maneuvers explained in other chapters including the formation of passing triangles, splitting the defense, penetrating on the dribble, committing the defense, and driving the baseline form the basic nature of this option in securing shots. The passing option takes advantage of individual shooting abilities and the use of percentage shooting via shooting spots.

The second option of the offense consists of sending a player through the zone to the basket and is appropriately called the cutter option. The techniques explained in earlier chapters which specifically apply to the cutter action include player rotation, pattern rotation, offensive penetration, weakside action, screening the zone, pattern continuity, overshifting the defense, cutting and reversing, and reversing the pass.

The third option of the offensive sets is the post or roll maneuver. The techniques specifically designed for use in this option

The Offensive Patterns in the Multiple Set Zone Offense

include the high post roll, low post roll, low post loop, post men exchange, and low post slide maneuvers.

In analyzing the various options of the five sets, there are certain similarities which aid in the learning process and simplify the movement patterns. In the passing options the primary purpose is movement of the ball to secure good percentage shooting situations. The player selected to perform the cutting action is determined by the set alignment. The sets involving a high post (1-3-1, 2-1-2, 1-3-1 overload) employ the first player from the ball to initiate the cut maneuver. This would be the wing man in the 1-3-1 and 1-3-1 overload, and the guard in the 2-1-2. Diagram

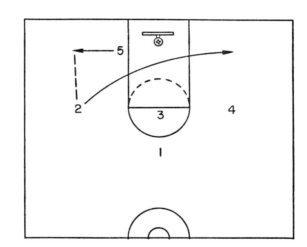

Diagram 5-1

5-1 shows the player responsible for initiating the cut in the sets employing a high post.

The sets not incorporating a high post (2-2-1, 3-2) employ the second man from the corner to initiate the cut maneuver. Diagram 5-2 shows the player responsible for cutting in set which does not use a high post.

The post options are all similar to the sets employing a high post in that the roll is performed immediately if the cutter does not initiate his action through the defense after the ball is passed into the corner.

THE 1-3-1 CUT AND ROLL SET

The 1-3-1 set utilizes a mobile high post man very effectively. It can be used against all even front zone defenses. Diagram 5-3 shows the initial positioning of the 1-3-1 set.

Player 1 is defined as the offensive point and initiates the offense from the top of the key. He assumes his basic position one-two steps off the circle depending on the type of defensive pressure employed. Players 2 and 4 are the wing men who operate at a forty-five degree angle from the basket. They position themselves eight-ten feet from the sideline even with the foul line

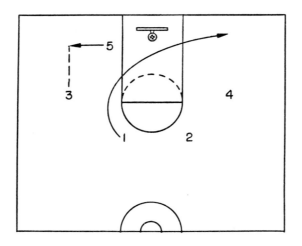

Diagram 5-2

extended. Player 3 is the high post operative and is stationed on the foul line. Player 5 is the single low post and can operate stationed on either side of the basket. He is even with the basket and tight on the foul lane. His position designates the strongside of the formation.

Passing Option

In this option rapid movement of the ball around the perimeter initially checks the defensive pressure and reaction. If the defense reacts and recovers poorly to the ball, spot shooting and penetration via the dribble become effective offensive maneuvers. It is important that all passes made are directed to the next player. This enables all players at least three passing possibilities to help eliminate defensive pressure. Player 1 may pass to players 2, 3, or 4. Player 2 may pass to 1, 3, or 5. Player 3 may pass to players 1, 2, or 4. He also is able on occasion to drop a pass off to 5 along the baseline. Player 4 may pass to players 1, 3, or 5. And player 5 may pass to players 2, 3, or 4. We discourage passes made which eliminate a player in the passing order. For example player 2 passing to 4. This prevents unnecessary lob passes and the ball being left up for grabs if the defense reacts quickly. The primary rebounders in this option are 3, 5, and the weakside wing at the time of the shot.

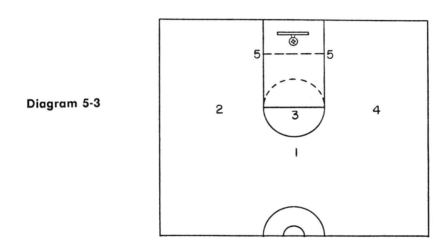

Diagram 5-3

The secondary rebounder and defender is the strongside wing. Player 1 is the safety valve on defense to prevent a long pass for an easy layup. Diagram 5-4 shows basic player positioning for the passing option in the 1-3-1 set and available passing lanes.

Cutter Option

The cutter option is initiated by passing from the wing position to the low post who moves to a wide position in the corner. The correct movement sequence is 2 passing to 5 in the corner. 2 cuts towards the basket looking for a return pass and then moves momentarily to a low post position on the weakside to see what develops. 3 rolls behind 2 down the lane looking for a quick pass from 5. If no passing lanes are open inside, 1 adjusts down to the wing position vacated by 2. 5 passes to 1 and 4 breaks to an open spot in the lane looking for a pass and shot. 4 has the option of timing his break into the lane when either 5 or 1 has the ball. Either can be successful depending on the defense and 4 through experience will determine when he should make his move. When nothing is available after this movement, one of two adjustments are made. 1 dribbles back to the point position and 4 continues across lane to become the strongside win, or 4 moves out to the point after his break into the lane and receives a pass from 1. The proper movement will

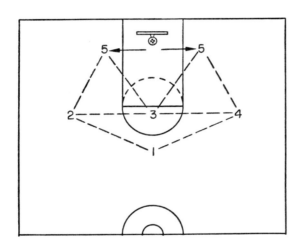

Diagram 5-4

be determined by the defensive action on 1 when he receives the ball in the wing position. 3 moves back to the high post and 2 slides up to the wing position. Diagram 5-5 shows the movement pattern of the cutter option.

After the cut has been completed, the ball is passed around the horn and 5 slides along the baseline to initiate the cutter option from the other side. The alternating action prevents the defense from anticipating the cut and keeps them honest in their shifting responsibilities. The primary rebounders are the cutter, low post, and high post. The secondary rebounder is the weakside wing moving into the lane area. The primary

The Offensive Patterns in the Multiple Set Zone Offense 69

defender is 1 who adjusts to maintain floor balance. Note the cutter being the first player from the corner when a high post set is utilized.

Roll Option

The roll option is determined by the action of the strongside wing. If the wing passes into the low post and holds his position, the roll option is in effect. 2 passes to 5 moving wide and stays. 3 rolls to the basket looking for a pass and continues across the lane. Immediately 4 breaks into the lane area as soon as 3 has cleared. This duo action of sending a man away from the ball and one back towards the ball is very effective. The

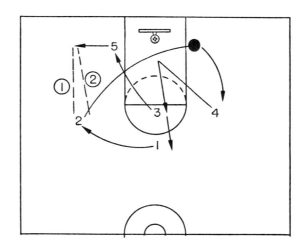

Diagram 5-5

player adjustments include 4 moving into the high post and 3 continuing out to the wing position vacated by 4. 5 passes back to 2. 2 passes to 1 on the point. If 4 is unable to operate from the high post position, 4 and 3 simply exchange when the ball is in the opposite wing or point position. Diagram 5-6 shows the player movement in the roll option.

The primary rebounders are the low post, high post, and the weakside wing. The secondary rebounder is the strongside wing. Player 1 is the primary defender against the break. The 1-3-1 cut and roll set is especially strong against the 2-1-2 and 2-3 zone defenses.

THE 2-1-2 PERIMETER SET

The 2-1-2 set is used to attack odd front zone defenses. Players 1 and 2 are the guards stationed one-two steps outside the top of the key about fifteen feet apart. 3 and 4 are the low post players stationed on either side of the foul lane even with the basket one step outside the lane. They will move higher and wider as the defensive pressure dictates. 5 is the high post stationed on the foul line. Diagram 5-7 shows player positioning in the 2-1-2 set.

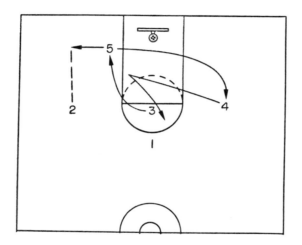

Diagram 5-6

Passing Option

In using the passing option, there is good balance in the 2-1-2 set because of the equal distribution of players on the floor. The offense will widen slightly causing the defense to spread out and consequently open up the high post area. Once again ball movement and penetration are important principles to succeed with the passing option. Diagram 5-8 shows the player positioning in the passing option of the 2-1-2 set.

The primary rebounders are 3, 4, and 5 which are already formed in a natural cup around the basket. The shooting guard is the secondary rebounder. The other guard away from the action is the primary defender.

Cutter Option

The presence of a high post automatically designates the first player from the corner which is the guard making the pass into the low post as the cutter. Therefore, 1 passes to 3 and starts his cutting maneuver through the defense and out to the opposite corner. 2 adjusts over to the area vacated by 1 and receives a pass back from 3. If the defense overplays 2 preventing the pass from being completed, 5 rolls from his high post position towards the ball for a possible pass and inside move. Generally however,

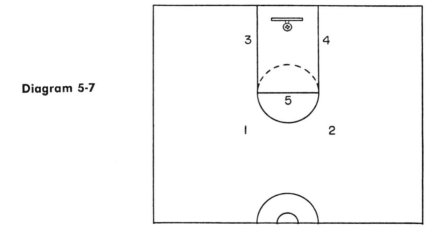

Diagram 5-7

the pass from 3 to 2 will be completed as the defense sags and closes off the middle. As 2 receives the ball, 5 pivots and backs out to the top of the key to receive a pass from 2. 4 moves into a tight position on the foul lane. 5 passes to 1 in the corner who immediately looks for a shot. If the defense recovers quickly on him in the corner, the pass is dropped off to 4 inside for a shot. If the defense makes a good adjustment on the corner (1), and fronts 4 preventing a pass inside, 5 quickly moves back into the high post area looking for a return pass and shot. Diagram 5-9 shows the cutter option in the 2-1-2 set.

The player adjustment involves 1 dribbling back to a guard position or passing to 2 moving back over and then moving out. The primary rebounders in the cutter option are 3, 4, and 5. The secondary rebounder is the guard in the corner after his cut. The primary defender is the guard remaining outside the top of the key.

Roll Option

The roll option is initiated by either guard passing into a low post and holding their position. This keys 5 to roll towards the basket down the lane and to assume a position tight on the lane away from the ball at the conclusion of his maneuver. As 5 clears, the low post loops to the basket for a possible pass and then returns back to the corner. 3 passes back to 1. 1 passes to 2. 2 passes to 4 in the corner for a shot or a pass inside to 5 on

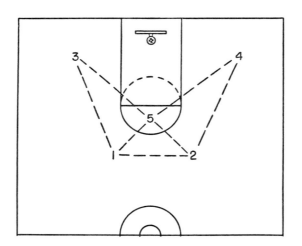

Diagram 5-8

the lane if the defense moves out to the corner for coverage. 4 can take the 15-18' jumper or pass inside to 5 for a power move. Diagram 5-10 shows the movement in the roll option of the 2-1-2 set.

Player adjustments include 5 moving back up to the high post to his original position. 4 moves back inside to his tight lane position. The primary rebounders are 3, 4, and 5. The guard passing in to initiate the roll is the primary defender. The other guard becomes the secondary defender or rebounder. The 2-1-2 set works especially well against a 1-2-2 or 3-2 zone defense.

The Offensive Patterns in the Multiple Set Zone Offense 73

Diagram 5-9

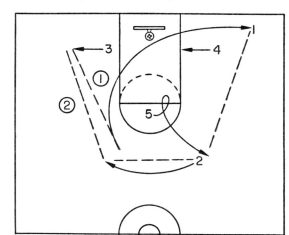

THE 3-2 BASELINE SCREEN SET

The 3-2 set is likewise used against all even front zone defenses as are the other odd front offensive sets. Player 1 is the point and is stationed one-two steps outside the top of the key. Players 2 and 3 are the wing men and positioned eight-ten feet from the sideline even with or one step above the foul line extended. Players 4 and 5 are the low posts and are stationed one step off the foul lane and even with the basket on either side of the basket. Diagram 5-11 shows the player distribution in the 3-2 set.

Passing Option

The passing option is initiated to check the defensive movement to the ball as in the other sets. However, the nature of this spread formation allows more open area in the lane. Ad-

Diagram 5-10

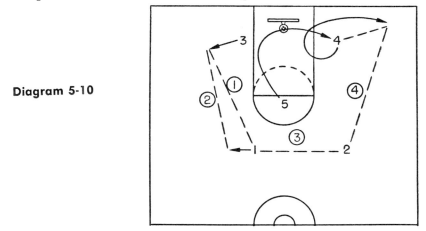

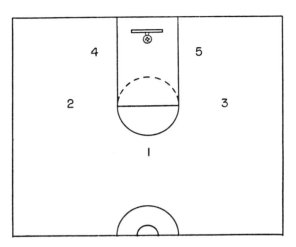

Diagram 5-11

ditional scoring opportunities are created by utilizing the base line more effectively through this option by incorporating player movement in the passing phase. The sequence of movements to initiate the baseline screen starts with a pass to either wing from the point position. The wing (2) receiving the ball starts on a dribble towards the baseline. The point (1) and the other wing (3) adjust and rotate towards the ball. This gives an appearance of a 2-3 formation. 2 looks for a shot or a possible pass inside to 4 when he reaches the baseline. If 4 is being fronted by a defender, 2 passes back to 1 who is now in the wing position.

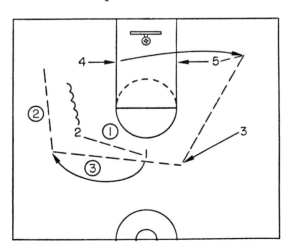

Diagram 5-12

The Offensive Patterns in the Multiple Set Zone Offense   75

1 passes to 3. 3 passes to 4 who has slid along the baseline using 5 as a screen and moving to the corner. 4 has the option of taking a shot if clear, or looking inside to 5 if the defender releases and moves out to the corner for coverage. Diagram 5-12 shows the initial movement pattern in the passing option. When neither opportunity is presented to 4 upon his pass reception in the corner, the second phase of the passing option goes into effect. The 2-3 formation is still in effect after the exchange of players. 4 passes back to 3. 3 passes to 1. 1 passes to 5 who moves from his tight lane position and slides along the baseline to the corner using 2, who adjusted to an inside position after his penetration as a screen. This three player involvement along the baseline can remain continuous indefinitely and actually resembles a delayed three-man weave. Diagram 5-13 shows the second phase of the passing option moving the ball back to the other side.

This option becomes extremely effective when the player assuming the tight lane position for the inside drop pass from the corner is mobile and possesses the ability to get the shot off in traffic. He becomes a tremendous scoring weapon inside the zone. In the passing option the primary rebounders are the three baseline players (4, 5 and either 2 or 3). The secondary rebounder is the guard on the opposite side the shot was taken from. The other guard is the primary defender.

Cutter Option

The cutter option is initiated by a pass from the wing position to a low post moving wide to a corner position. As 2 passes to 4, 1 cuts from his point position through the middle and out to the opposite corner. After 1 clears, 5 loops toward the ball into the lane and back to his original position if he does not receive the ball. The ball is then reversed from 4 back to 2. 2 passes to 3 adjusting over. 3 quickly passes to 1 in the corner. 1 looks immediately for a shot or pass to 5 inside on the lane. The absence of a shooting opportunity brings 1 on a dribble out to the wing position and passes to 3 on the point to begin the cutter option to either side. Diagram 5-14 shows the player action in the cutter option of the 3-2 set.

Note as mentioned previously that the second player from the ball is the cutter in the sets without a high post in operation.

The primary rebounders are the cutter and both low post players. The secondary rebounder is the guard opposite the side a shot is taken from. The primary defender is the other side.

Roll Option

A high post does not exist in the 3-2 set and consequently the roll maneuver is performed by one of the low post players. Either 4 or 5 moves to a semi-high side position half way between the basket and the foul line. The low post assuming this position is determined by the side of the floor the ball is brought up. 3 advances the ball up the right side and this action keys 5, who is on the same side, to move to the semi-high

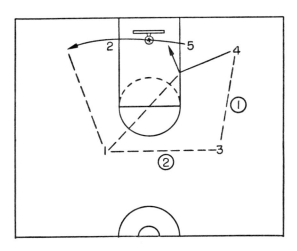

Diagram 5-13

position. 3 looks to pass inside to 5 for a turn around jump shot if he is open. With nothing available, 3 passes to 1 on the point. 1 passes to 2. 2 passes to 4 moving wide to receive a pass. 4 immediately looks for 5 rolling from his semi-high position to deliver a pass inside the zone or has the opportunity for a baseline jumper. Diagram 5-15 shows the player movement in the roll option.

The player adjustment for this option is simply 5 moving back across the lane to his original position. The roll option is only attempted once each time down the floor to eliminate confusion by the players as well as one of the wing players standing around dribbling the ball waiting for the low post to

The Offensive Patterns in the Multiple Set Zone Offense 77

move up. It is an easy task to move immediately into either the passing or cutting option. The primary rebounders in the roll option are both low post men and the wing opposite the ball. The secondary rebounder is the wing on the same side of the ball. The primary defender is the point player. The 3-2 set works especially well against a 2-3 zone.

THE 2-2-1 WEAKSIDE SLIDE SET

The 2-2-1 set is used against all odd front zone defenses. Players 1 and 2 are the guards positioned one-two steps beyond the top of the key about fifteen feet apart. Players 3 and 4 are the forwards stationed in the wing positions about ten feet in

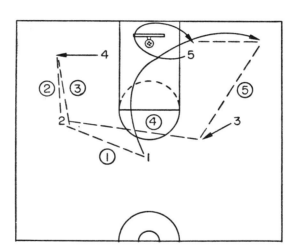

Diagram 5-14

from the sideline even with the foul line extended. These two positions will vary according to the defensive pressure applied. 5 is the low post stationed on either side of the foul lane even with the basket and roams the baseline as the ball moves around the perimeter of the defense. Diagram 5-16 shows the basic positioning of players in the 2-2-1 set.

Passing Option

The passing option allows for quick ball movement and penetration. All five players are involved as the ball moves around the perimeter of the defense. Many opportunities for shots are presented. As the ball is passed from guard to guard,

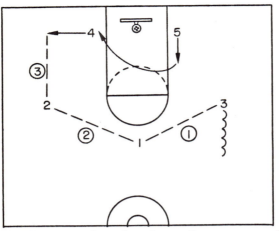

Diagram 5-15

the low post has freedom of movement into the lane area to split the low defenders looking for a pass and power move around the basket. As the ball moves to the wing position, the opposite wing man filters through the defense into an open spot in the lane momentarily looking for a pass and close shot. Finally, as the ball is passed into the low post the guard opposite flashes into the foul line looking for a pass and 15' jump shot. Diagram 5-17 shows the movement possibilities of the players in the 2-2-1 set. The primary rebounders are the low post player and both wing players. The secondary rebounder is

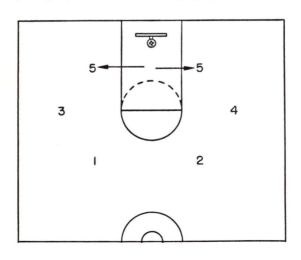

Diagram 5-16

the guard opposite the side the shot was taken. The primary defender is the other guard.

Cutter Option

The cutter option is initiated by either wing player passing into a low post moving wide to the corner. 1 passes to 3. 3 passes to 5. The absence of a high post designates the second player from the ball performing the cut maneuver to the basket. If 1 does not receive the ball, he continues out to the corner opposite the ball. After 1 clears the lane area, the weakside wing (in this case 4) filters through the defense across the lane looking for a pass from 5. When neither opportunity exists,

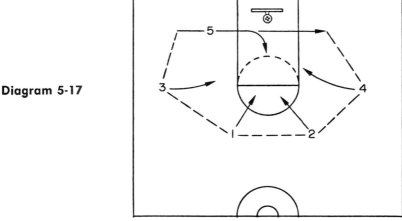

Diagram 5-17

5 passes back to 3. 3 passes to 2 adjusting to the top of the key. 2 passes to 1 stationed in the corner for the shot. Diagram 5-18 shows the movement of the cutter option in the 2-2-1 set. The player adjustments include 1 moving to the wing position vacated by 4 after passing back outside to 2. 3 adjusts to become the other guard with 2. 4 continues out to the wing position vacated by 3. 2 can then pass back around the perimeter to initiate the cut again, or reverse a pass back to 1. 1 passes to 5 sliding along the baseline to initiate the cutter option with the second man away going through.

The primary rebounders are the low post and both wing men.

The secondary rebounder is the cutter moving through. The primary defender is the other guard remaining outside.

Roll Option

The roll option is keyed by the guard bringing the ball into front court down the sideline. The low post (5) moves to a semi-high post on the same side as the ball. After initially looking inside for 5, the ball is passed laterally to the other guard. He passes the ball into the wing position. As the wing receives the ball, the post rolls from his semi-high position

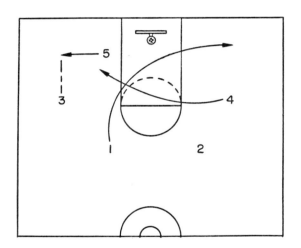

Diagram 5-18

across the lane to the basket. Diagram 5-19 shows the player movement in the post option of the 2-2-1 set.

As 5 clears the high post area on his roll, this is an excellent time for the weakside wing to perform a looping maneuver into the high post area and back looking for a quick look-in pass. If a defensive overplay prevents a pass from 4 back to 2 after 5 rolls, 4 passes back to 5 who moves wide and 2 cuts to the basket, keeping the continuity of the offense in operation. The primary rebounders are the low post and the two wing players. The strong side guard becomes the safety valve against the break while the weakside guard becomes either a secondary rebounder or assists for defensive purposes. The 2-2-1 set is especially effective against the 1-3-1 zone defense.

THE 1-3-1 OVERLOAD SET

This particular set takes advantage of individual shooting abilities from the wing positions and can be used at times against all forms of zone defenses. 1 is the best ball handling guard and plays the point position one-two steps outside the top of the key. The strongside wing is played by the best shooter and takes a position splitting the high and low post players

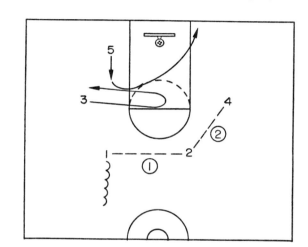

Diagram 5-19

about 8' from the sideline. The weakside wing is played by a forward stationed on the foul lane splitting the distance between the high and low post positions.

The high post is played by the most mobile big man who has the ability to turn and take the jump shot. He is stationed on the edge of the foul line and foul circle facing the strongside wing. The low post is occupied by the center. He takes a position on the foul lane even with the basket and also faces the strong side wing. Diagram 5-20 shows the player positioning in the 1-3-1 overload set.

Passing Option

This is the most often used option in this set with the main idea of utilizing the best shooter on the team in the strongside wing position. Basically the ball movement will open up many shooting opportunities from both weak and strongside wing positions and also passing into the high post for quick turn around jumpers. Many two-men situations develop to put pressure on a single defensive player. They include: the point and strongside action, the point and high post action, strongside wing and high post, and the strongside wing and low post action. Experience has shown the greatest number of shots taken are from the strongside wing. As the defense shifts to cover the strongside, the position most important is the high post who will be free momentarily because of the overplay on the wing. The

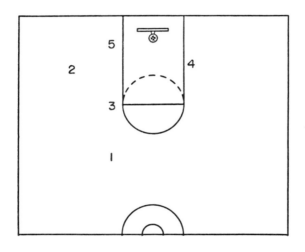

Diagram 5-20

low post freezes the low defender from reacting out to the ball and is the primary offensive rebounder for second efforts on missed shots. The weakside wing is a safety valve and picks up a lot of points around the basket because of the basic closeness of his position. Diagram 5-21 shows the passing lane availabilities in the 1-3-1 overload set.

The primary rebounders are the low post, high post, and weakside wing. The strongside wing is a secondary rebounder and defender. The point player is the primary defender.

The Offensive Patterns in the Multiple Set Zone Offense 83

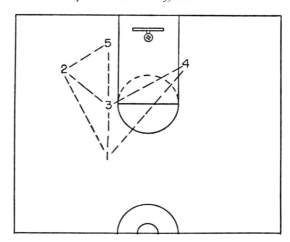

Diagram 5-21

Cutter Option

The cut maneuver is initiated by the low post (5) moving wide to receive a pass from the strongside wing (2) who is being pressured. 2 cuts to the basket after his pass. 3 moves from the high post to the strongside position vacated to receive a pass back from 5. The weakside wing (4) breaks to the open spot in the lane by filtering through the defense from behind and moving to the high post position vacated by 3. 3 looks for 4 and then passes back to the point (1). After the pass 3 and 4 exchange to move 3 back inside to the high post position. Diagram 5-22 shows the player movement in the cutter option of the overload set.

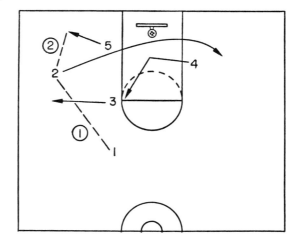

Diagram 5-22

The primary rebounders are the high post, low post, and the weakside wing after the cut. The point player is the primary defender. The strongside wing is the secondary defender and rebounder.

Roll Option

The post roll maneuver is initiated by a pass to the weakside wing (4) from the point (1). To receive the pass the weakside wing moves to a wider position, preventing a defender from closing off the passing lane from 1. After the pass, 3 rolls from his high post position towards the ball and takes a low post

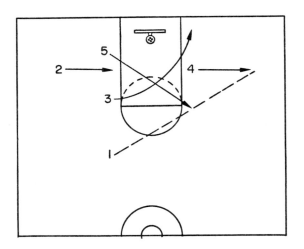

Diagram 5-23

position on the ball side. As 3 clears through the middle, 5 moves from the low post towards the ball looking for an open spot and then to the high post position vacated. 2 moves into a tight lane position to become the weakside wing as the strongside of the overload is shifted with the roll option. Diagram 5-23 illustrates the player movement in the roll option of the overload set.

The roll option not only creates inside movement but also allows the strongside of the set to change without moving players around individually. The primary rebounders remain the same with the low post, high post and weakside wing as-

The Offensive Patterns in the Multiple Set Zone Offense   85

suming this responsibility. The secondary rebounder and defender is the strongside wing. The point player once again is the primary defender. The 1-3-1 overload set is extremely versatile but is most effective against a 2-1-2 and 2-3 zone defense.

SUMMARY OF PRINCIPLES

The material presented in discussing the component parts of the multiple set seem very complex at first analysis. However, once the basic concepts are grasped the same actions and reactions are repeated, only in different areas on the floor. In condensing the principles to approach incorporating the multiple set offense the total picture is cleared up considerably.

1. Each set employs three options. They are a passing option, cutter option, and a roll option.
2. The passing option of each set is concerned primarily with ball movement around the perimeter of the defense to gain good percentage shooting opportunities. No major adjustments are made and the passing concepts remain the same although the positions of the players are changed depending on the set used. The abilities to move the ball quickly and penetrate when openings exist are primary sources of securing scoring opportunities in this option.
3. The cutter option in each set is based on a slicing maneuver towards the basket after a pass has been made to a low post player in the corner. In the sets employing a high post (1-3-1, 1-3-1 overload, 2-1-2), the player passing to the corner cuts. In the sets without a high post (2-2-1, 3-2), the second player from the corner performs the cut.
4. The roll option in each set revolves around a similar post maneuver, that of rolling towards the ball and basket for a possible pass reception inside the defense. All rolling action is initiated by the wing player or guard passing to the corner and holding his position.

A few closing comments are necessary to use the multiple set to its full potential. We have never employed all five sets in any one game. Depending on our current scouting report, past scouting reports, and zone tendencies of the opponent we are facing, our game play is formulated around using the sets we feel necessary to achieve success. Generally we approach each game with three sets in mind. One even front set, one odd front set, and the 1-3-1 overload set are used in our game preparation preceeding each opponent. An example will help clarify this thinking. We always have our overload on hand to take advantage of specialized shooting abilities. If we are playing a team that uses a 2-1-2 zone, the sets to include along with the overload are the 1-3-1 and the 2-2-1. The 2-1-2 zone is weak in the wing areas and the three sets selected are very strong in that particular area. If the point player in the 1-3-1 is pressured extremely well by the two defensive guards causing the offense to bog down, we shift to the 2-2-1. This still allows us strength in the wing areas and also allows us a one to one match-up in the guard area, preventing any form of double teaming. Against a team employing a 2-3 zone, the counter maneuver includes utilizing the 1-3-1 set and 2-1-2 set to take advantage of the weakness in the high post area along with the overload for specialized shooting abilities. Although three sets are emphasized for each opponent, all five sets are at hand whenever the situation warrants the need and use of the complete multiple set system.

CHAPTER SIX

Automatic Maneuvers in the Multiple Set Zone Offense

An automatic maneuver is an action created by a defensive stunt. It becomes an immediate reaction to the defense and is a complement to the normal offensive pattern. At times the stunting action and anticipation of the defense prevents the normal flow of the offensive pattern from continuing. To counteract these defensive tactics, there are corresponding reactions the offense can use to regain an advantage.

As the specialized options of the offensive pattern are forming the defense may react by overshifting, attempting to trap, pressuring the ball, sagging to close off any cutting action, or anticipating the next pass for the steal. It then becomes necessary for the offense to react to the defensive movement in place of forcing the designated option. These automatic responses can be more effective than the intended options if run properly.

Automatic maneuvers do not just happen. They must be practiced daily and re-emphasized each time the situation arises. Players must be constantly reminded each time an automatic action would have been the logical choice in place

88   Automatic Maneuvers in the Multiple Set Zone Offense

of the intended option. Repetition is the key to forming good habits. Some teams base their entire offensive system on individual moves and developing automatic reactions for different defensive pressure situations. However devised or incorporated, the use of automatics is an integral part in developing a successful offensive system of play.

REVERSING THE PASS

The most fundamental automatic maneuver in developing offensive pressure against zone defenses is a technique called reversing the pass. It takes advantage of the defensive flow in a single direction as they are pursuing the ball. All zone defenses are similar in that the players shift together in reacting to the movement of the ball. As this occurs there is a tendency by the defense in many cases to overshift in anticipation of the ball movement. When this happens making it difficult to complete the subsequent pass, it becomes advantageous to immediately change the direction of the ball by reversing the pass back to its original position. This can catch the defense off balance and produce a good shooting opportunity. This technique becomes particularly effective when employing a cutting option. An example of this maneuver can be shown by utilizing the 2-2-1 set against a 1-3-1 zone defense. Diagram 6-1 illustrates the basic movement of the set and the action described as reversing the pass.

The cut option originates with a pass from the wing man (3) to the low post (5) moving out to the corner. For simplicity and less confusion in the diagram, the ball is established in the low post position. The cutter (1) who is the second player from the ball cuts towards the basket and out to the opposite corner. If the cutter is not open, the ball is passed back to the wing. The completion of the option consists of passing the ball around the horn from 3 to 2 to the cutter in the corner for a jump shot. As this particular option continues to be run the defense will become accustomed to the movement of the cutter and will have a tendency to anticipate the passing action around the horn and adjust accordingly by quickly shifting to cover the cutter in the corner. Therefore as the ball moves on its normal course from 5 to 3 to 2 adjusting, the reverse passing action comes into play. Player 2, detecting the defense overplaying the cutter in the

Automatic Maneuvers in the Multiple Set Zone Offense 89

corner and anticipating the pass, fakes in and reverses the pass back to the wing (3). Oftentimes this will catch the defense out of position to react because of their preliminary anticipation of the pass going into the corner. Consequently the wing will be open for a shot or pass quickly to the low post for a baseline jumper.

This reverse pass technique is also performed successfully in the passing options by employing a single direction ball movement around the entire perimeter of the defense. This will lull the defense into lethargic shifting in the same direction following the systematic movement of the ball. After a number of passes around the defense, a player fakes in the same direction

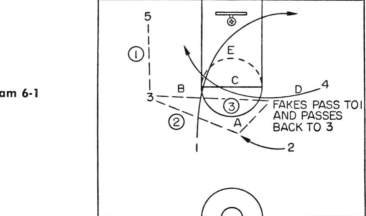

Diagram 6-1

and reverses a pass in the opposite direction. In the majority of cases the defense will be caught flat-footed and the result is a temporary opening for a shot.

RELEASING AND MOVING

Releasing and moving is a technique designed to keep the defense off balance. It prevents the defense from applying additional pressure on the ball along with making them exert extra effort to cover all the possibilities that will exist. The elements of this technique include:

1. Passing and cutting to the basket sharply, always looking for a return pass.

90   *Automatic Maneuvers in the Multiple Set Zone Offense*

2. Passing and faking in to give the impression of cutting, and stepping back for a return pass and possible shot.
3. Passing and exchanging with other players to check the defensive movement.
4. Passing and moving to an open spot behind or between the defense.

Each of these maneuvers keeps the entire defense active and not able to concentrate on any one or two specific players. Releasing a pass and moving also minimizes the effectiveness of the defense to overplay the receiver, pressure the ball, anticipate passes, or gamble out of position for a possible steal. Zone defenses generally react poorly or lazily with footwork due to the fact that other players are ready to pick up the ball. Therefore, player movement as well as ball movement are effective techniques against zone defenses.

CUTTING AND REVERSING

The cut and reverse maneuver is the second phase or additional action of the cutter going to the basket. It is very effective when used sparingly and at the proper time. In the majority of situations in which a player cuts to the basket he fails to receive a return pass. There are three reasons why this occurs. In the first place the zone defense initially covers the cutter very tightly and the risk involved in completing a pass in the lane area is a poor percentage move. Second, the cutter after performing the cut two or three times becomes discouraged because he is not receiving a pass. Therefore, oftentimes a player cuts without paying any attention to a return pass. Third, due to the inability of a player to complete a pass the cutter may develop a poor tendency of jogging through the middle. The sharpness and threat of the cut maneuver is then minimized. The result is the player only cuts because the coach or offense dictates the maneuver. Because the pure cut becomes ineffective as a scoring threat, something must be added to the basic cut maneuver. The reverse step action is the necessary addition to make the basic cut a scoring threat.

The cutting action against zone defenses is divided into three phases.

Automatic Maneuvers in the Multiple Set Zone Offense 91

1. The penetration pass and initial step or two to pop the offensive player behind the first line of defensive players.
2. The cutter continues on a straight line course to the basket.
3. The conclusion of the cut occurs around the basket where the passing angle is completely closed off.

At this time the defense once again concentrates on the ball and forgets about the cutter. This is when the reverse action comes into play. Instead of continuing to the opposite corner immediately after reaching the basket, the cutter reverses his

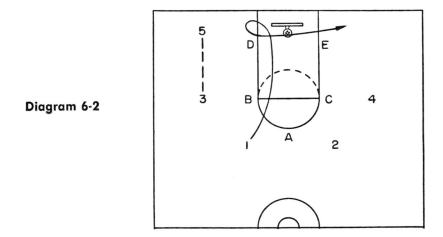

Diagram 6-2

direction and takes one to two steps back towards the ball along the baseline once again looking for a pass. Oftentimes this maneuver will catch the defense napping. If the pass is not there immediately, the cutter momentarily pauses and continues on his normal route to the opposite corner. His instructions if he is able to receive a pass on the reverse maneuver inside are to get the shot off and attempt to draw a foul. Diagram 6-2 shows the path of the cutter in the 2-2-1 set and reverse cutting action at the basket along the baseline against a 3-2 zone.

PENETRATING THE BASELINE

A fundamental rule against zone defenses is to keep the ball moving and only dribble as a last resort. This will occur when the passing lanes are closed or cut off. However, an effective maneuver can be developed by penetrating along the baseline on a dribble. The opportunity is possible dependent upon the type of coverage supplied by the low defender.

The cut option in all the sets is initiated by a pass to the low post moving out to the corner. The defensive adjustment is to rush the corner or give up a good percentage shot from 15'. When the situation occurs, the defender is primarily concerned with pressuring the ball and oftentimes forgets basic defensive rules applying to protecting the baseline. Consequently he may be out of position and off balance. In this awkward position he is prone to a head and shoulder fake. The result can be a dribble penetration along the baseline for a subsequent shot or a pass to a teammate in a better position to shoot. Three scoring possibilities are developed by the baseline penetration against a zone. The first opportunity is presented as the defender is initially beaten along the baseline for a short jump shot. A normal defensive cover up brings the other low defender over to prevent further penetration. The second opportunity is developed by the weakside wing sliding along the baseline towards the ball and basket. If the defensive middle man reacts quick enough to close him off, the high post moves to an open spot in the lane area to receive a pass to complete the third scoring possibility. The high post must not get over anxious and move to soon before the middle defender releases his coverage to adjust. Otherwise, a three-second violation may be the result from poor timing. Diagrams 6-3, 6-4, and 6-5 show the three scoring possibilities developed by penetrating the baseline. The example is based on movement of the 1-3-1 set against a 2-1-2 zone defense.

FAKING AND PENETRATING

This automatic maneuver is effective when the defense is forced to rush directly at an offensive player. The situation is created by passing the ball from area to area forcing a change in the defensive responsibility rather than just a slide step by

Automatic Maneuvers in the Multiple Set Zone Offense 93

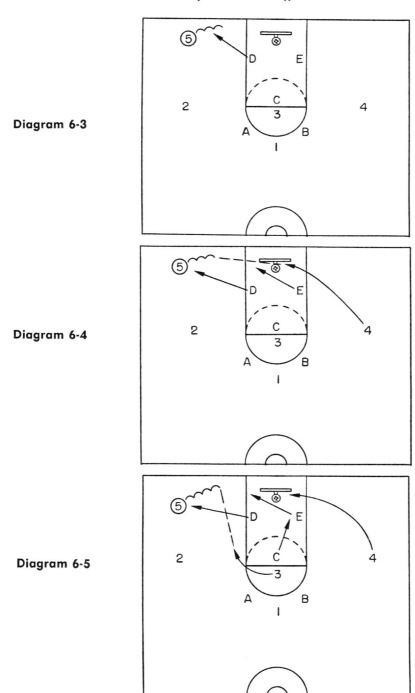

Diagram 6-3

Diagram 6-4

Diagram 6-5

a single player for coverage. A pass from guard to guard in the even front sets and point to high post in the odd front sets are examples of situations which do not require major changes in defensive responsibility. But there are a number of situations which force a change in responsibility and a straight-on approach for coverage by the defense to enable this action of faking and penetrating to take place. Three such passing exchanges which encourage defensive head-on coverage to produce this action are:

1. A pass from the wing position to the corner. This forces the low defender to rush the corner to prevent a 15-18' shot. Using the proper faking technique the offensive player can penetrate along the baseline or to the inside looking for a closer shooting opportunity or further penetration.
2. A return pass from the corner to the wing position forces the defensive guard or forward to charge him. If the offensive wing stays alert it is possible to penetrate for a shot, penetrate and pass back to the low post, or penetrate and pass off to another teammate sliding into the spot vacated by the defender.
3. A pass from the high post to the wing position forces the defense to move out after sagging on the high post. The same penetration principles mentioned above are once again presented to the wing man.

A summary of passing situations in the different sets that force the defense to apply head-on pressure and consequently allow the offensive player the option of faking and penetrating are:

1. 1-3-1 Cut and Roll Set
   A. Wing passing to low post
   B. Low post passing to wing
   C. High post passing to wing
   D. High post passing to low post
2. 2-1-2 Perimeter Set
   A. Guard passing to low post
   B. Low post passing to guard
   C. High post passing to guard
   D. High post passing to low post

Automatic Maneuvers in the Multiple Set Zone Offense 95

   3. 3-2 Baseline Screen Set
      A. Wing passing to low post
      B. Low post passing to wing
   4. 2-2-1 Weakside Slide Set
      A. Wing passing to low post
      B. Low post passing to wing
      C. Guard passing to wing
      D. Wing passing to guard
   5. 1-3-1 Overload Set
      A. Wing passing to low post
      B. Low Post passing to wing
      C. High post passing to strongside wing
      D. Point passing to weakside wing

SHOOTING AND FOLLOWING

Following the shot is basic to offensive theory, but one of the toughest individual skills to teach. Players will respond to this skill differently. Some players form a good habit in taking all their shots in good balance, enabling them to consistently become an offensive threat on second efforts. Other players will shoot off balance and only follow occasionally. Regardless of the ability of individual players, each player can improve himself in this particular area.

In many cases the defender is out of position to screen out after the shot is taken. He is either leaving the floor on the shot or making a last ditch effort to rush the shooter. Consequently the shooter must be a primary rebounder for two reasons. Because the defender may be out of position on the shot, the path following the shot may be wide open giving the shooter a tremendous advantage to get the rebound. Second, the shooter normally will have the best idea where the missed shot will rebound and should be able to get there quickest.

In developing the area of shooting and following there are certain elements to be considered. In the first place players must be instructed to shoot their shot in complete body balance. To accomplish this the shooter must be landing in approximately the same spot he took off from or at least moving towards the basket when he lands. We feel there are three reasons why it is difficult for many players to perfect the skill of following

96 *Automatic Maneuvers in the Multiple Set Zone Offense*

their own shot. First of all some players develop a tendency to fade away when developing their shooting technique. It becomes very hard to break a habit that has taken years to form. Second, many shots are taken on the move and consequently the body is moving to the left or right after the shot. Finally, a shot looks beautiful when observing it from a stationary position. Players enjoy watching the flight of the ball and do not want to expend the necessary effort in getting it back. In improving the skill of the shooter following his shot there are three specific drills we use.

1. Body Position Drill

This drill consists of taping or chalking a circle on the floor with an 18 inch diameter. Each player attempts stationary jump shots to determine their landing position after the shot. If a player is guilty of fading away on a stationary jump shot outside of the boundaries of the circle, a correction must be made. The coach will position himself behind the boy just outside the circle. As the player starts falling back after his release of the shot, the coach gently braces him in the back to force him to land in the same general area he took off from. This helps to reinforce the idea of proper shooting balance to the players. After this technique is mastered, the players attempt jump shots off the dribble moving forward, left and right. The movement is to the circle area to check the amount of floating motion at the completion of the shot. The emphasis is to stabilize the body as much as possible to be in position to follow the shot immediately after landing.

2. Momentary Delay Drill

As the players master the technique of jumping and landing in balance ready to react, the next phase is moving quickly and effectively to the basket. Some players will start movement so quickly that the result will be a poor finish on the follow through of the shot or a miscalculation of the direction of the rebound. The players in this drill are instructed to finish the follow through, land and momentarily watch the flight of the ball before they move after it. The drill is set up with a single line of players about eighteen feet from the basket. The coach

Automatic Maneuvers in the Multiple Set Zone Offense 97

or manager shoots the ball and each player in order waits until the ball hits the rim. The players then attempt to react and grab the ball before it hits the floor. The drill continues from the five general areas on the court including the key, left wing, right wing, left corner, and right corner. This part of the drill serves two purposes. The first is to teach the players to watch the flight of the ball momentarily in relation to the basket. The second purpose is to give the players some insight into the direction the ball will generally rebound off the rim from the different positions. There have been studies showing the percentage of rebounds going in certain directions off the rim from specific areas on the floor. These are valuable in showing general tendencies of rebounds. However, we feel that a player should experience as much as possible the actual rebound off the rim. The second phase of the drill is to allow the players to shoot the shot and follow to retrieve the ball before it hits the floor. The emphasis is on total completion of the shot from takeoff to follow-through before moving in for the offensive rebound.

3. Shot Reaction Drill

The third drill to improve following the shot is organized by breaking the squad down into pairs and using all available baskets. One player is the shooter positioned 15-18' from the basket and moving around the perimeter for consecutive shots. The second player is the rebounder and is stationed under the basket. The rebounder passes the ball to the shooter for jump shots. As long as the ball goes in they remain in their same positions as shooter and rebounder. When the shot is missed, the shooter must move to the basket and grab the ball before it hits the floor. The two players then reverse their positions as shooter and rebounder on a miss. If the shooter fails to rebound the missed shot before it hits the floor, laps or sprints can be assessed or any other suitable form of penalty for poor reaction. The reason for a penalty is to prevent the players from using this drill as a resting period and to concentrate on the purpose of the drill.

DEVELOPING THE SECOND EFFORT

The zone defense is excellent in terms of defensive rebounding. This of course is due to the positioning of the players along with the knowledge that there are always two or three defenders around the basket for the rebound. Offensively the opportunity for a second effort does not present itself as often as it would against a man for man defense. Consequently, it is imperative that the players take advantage of as many second effort opportunities as possible. Our players are instructed on an offensive rebound inside the lane area to immediately go back up for the shot. The movement is up and towards the basket. Only in rare situations will the ball be passed back outside. To consider the second effort successful one of three things must occur. The first and most desirable is a three-point play. Second, a basket, or third at the very least a foul on the defender and resultant foul shots.

In the majority of cases contact is an integral part of the action around the basket. Because of this we employ two drills designed to supply contact and familiarize the players with this possibility. The first drill is labeled "Double Team Layup Drill" and was fully explained in the chapter on shooting techniques. The second drill is called the "Animal Drill." The entire squad is placed in groups of three at different baskets. One ball is used in each group. The boundary lines for the drill are the foul line, endline, and foul lanes. The ball is given to one of the players to start the action. On command from the coach, the ball is tossed at the basket. Action continues for a period of time prescribed by the coach. Generally one minute time periods are more than sufficient. The ability to score baskets from close range in traffic revolves around the toughness of players to secure stray rebounds. The player with the ball momentarily is assigned as the offensive player while the other two are the defenders attempting to prevent the second effort. Each time the ball is put back up the responsibilities of the players change. The player gaining the rebound automatically becomes offense and the remaining two defense. Regardless of whether a basket is scored or not there is no break in the action until the coach signifies the drill is over. The player scoring the most baskets in the alloted time is determined the winner. An important note is to have players of like abilities competing at each station to get full benefit out of the challenging and aggressive aspect of this drill.

CHAPTER SEVEN

Breakdown Drills to Develop the Multiple Set Zone Offense

The theory behind breakdown drills is to emphasize proper timing and execution by isolating different elements of each specific option. In order to learn, repetition is essential. Repetition firmly plants in the minds of the players the proper movement pattern desired. This is particularly significant in learning offensive patterns. Players can perform and improve fundamental skills through individual work and practice. Learning offensive patterns correctly and efficiently requires additional players to benefit through the experience. These experiences to be valuable must be practiced and repeated daily in a variety of ways. One method is through half and full court scrimmage sessions. A second method involves scrimmages against other teams. A third method is actual game experience. A fourth method is to learn the patterns through a series of breakdown drills specifically designed from the complete pattern. Breakdown drills can aid the learning process more effectively by utilizing only the players who are actively involved in the specific maneuver of each option. Four reasons for employing the concept of breakdown drills include:

1. Continuous and concentrated repetition of a drill

100   *Breakdown Drills to Develop the Multiple Set Zone Offense*

situation enables the option to be learned easier, faster, and more effectively.

2. All players are kept active in a learning situation. It eliminates players from standing on the sideline during a scrimmage and also eliminates the inactive player or players in a particular option which are not currently involved in the flow of the play.

3. Breakdown drills build confidence. Players lose confidence in themselves and the system when mistakes are made in a scrimmage or they cannot operate effectively because the defense anticipates the offensive movement. This generally occurs when a lot of half court scrimmage situations are run. Players must achieve a degree of success to gain confidence. Breakdown drills give the players total knowledge about the complete pattern.

4. Breakdown drills give a different perspective to the players along with providing a change of pace from the constant routine of half and full court scrimmage sessions. Therefore, the interest level and motivation of the players is increased.

It is much easier on the coach and more fun for the players to scrimmage for most of the practice devoted to developing the offensive system of play. However, success does not come easily and certainly not by having a lot of fun. It takes hard work by everybody involved, especially the coach in his practice organization. Instituting breakdown drills takes a great deal of analysis and preparation on the part of the coach away from the practice floor. He must employ each member of the squad in a learning situation to achieve the end result desired. Breakdown drills segment different parts of the offense for concentration. Consequently they involve two, three, and four player situations in both a dummy and defensive setting.

PERIMETER PASSING

The passing options of all the sets involve certain basic similarities. The ball is passed quickly and accurately. Second, each player faces the basket on the pass reception to become

Breakdown Drills to Develop the Multiple Set Zone Offense 101

an offensive scoring threat. Third, there are basic offensive maneuvers that can be performed when receiving a pass.

1. Receive a pass, fake, and take a stationary jump shot.
2. Receive a pass, fake, penetrate the front line defense on a dribble and pull up for the shot.
3. Receive a pass, fake, and penetrate the front line defense to drive all the way to the basket.
4. Receive a pass, fake, penetrate the front line defense to draw the back line defense up and pass off to a teammate underneath the basket.
5. Receive a pass and continue the normal flow of the ball around the perimeter of the defense.
6. Receive a pass and reverse the flow of the ball to catch the defense anticipating the next pass.

Situations are incorporated to isolate two, three, and four players in a breakdown situation to improve these areas along with shooting accuracy. Two player situations are outlined in Chapter Eleven on shooting techniques. The three and four man situations are set up in the following manner. Enough baskets are used to employ all members of the squad with a minimum amount of time spent on the sideline watching. The result is that all players remain active most of the time and more opportunity for shooting improvement exists. Variety is introduced by organizing different shooting orders and direction of the ball movement. The drills are organized by placing the players in designated positions on the floor depending on the option emphasized and the number of players involved in the action.

1. The ball is passed rapidly between the players. On a whistle from the coach, the player next receiving the pass immediately sets himself in balance to take the shot. All the players converge on the rebound and tap it in if the shot was missed. The player getting to the ball first after the shot is replaced by an additional player who was assigned to that basket for the drill.
2. The ball is passed clockwise or counter clockwise. When the pass reaches the last player in the group, he takes the shot and follows for the tip in. He then dribbles to the front position of the group, the other players rotating one position. The passing continues with the last

player taking the shot, following and rotating one position after he dribbles back out.

3. The ball is passed clockwise or counter-clockwise a designated number of passes by the coach. Upon completion of the last pass, the player receiving the ball shoots and follows for the tip in. He dribbles back to his position and starts passing again. Each player receives the same number of shooting attempts.

The three-player situations used in the 1-3-1 set include 1-2-3, 1-3-4, 2-3-5, and 3-4-5. The four player situations include 1-2-3-4, 1-2-3-5, and 1-3-4-5.

The three-player situations used in the 2-1-2 set include 1-2-5, 1-3-5, 2-4-5, and 3-4-5. The four-player situations include 1-2-3-5 and 1-2-4-5.

The three-player situations used in the 3-2 set include 1-2-3, 1-2-4, and 1-3-5. The four-player situations include 1-2-3-4 and 1-2-3-5.

The three-player situations developed in the 2-2-1 set include 1-2-3, 1-2-4, 1-3-5, and 2-4-5. The four-player situations include 1-2-3-4, 1-2-3-5, and 1-2-4-5.

The three-player situations developed in the 1-3-1 overload set include 1-2-3, 1-3-4, and 2-3-5. The four-player situations include 1-2-3-4 and 1-3-4-5.

Referral to diagrams in previous chapters will furnish the positioning and numbers of the players in each set to develop the passing breakdown drills.

OFFENSIVE CUTTING ACTION

The progression for all the offensive cutting action is the same. The maneuvers are performed first in a dummy situation without any defense to insure the proper movement pattern being learned. Second, defense is only applied to the player receiving the pass and becoming the feeder. This enables the player to develop a series of fakes in coming to meet the pass. It is essential a player learn how to free himself from a denial or overplay defense to initiate the offensive action. The third step is to apply defense to the cutter emphasizing the importance of the first step on a cutting maneuver. And finally, defense is

Breakdown Drills to Develop the Multiple Set Zone Offense 103

presented to all players involved in the breakdown drill to simulate actual game conditions.

In explaining the 2, 3 and 4 man breakdown drills to improve the offensive cutting phase, individual diagrams are omitted to avoid unnecessary repetition of player positioning in the various sets. By referring to the chapter explaining the multiple set patterns, the positioning of the players is already stated along with the movement sequence. Therefore, a quick review will help cement the terminology and available options to be strengthened through the use of breakdown drills.

In the 1-3-1 set the players are divided into guards and forwards in breaking down the two-man situations. The guard assumes the wing position and passes into the forward moving wide from the low post position. After passing he performs his cut for a return pass and layup. A variation is for the forward to fake the pass and take the corner jump shot. After the two players work their action they move to the end of their respective lines. The three-player situation involves a high post, wing, and low post. The wing passes to the corner and cuts. After the wing clears, the high post rolls to the ball. Variations include passing to the cutter, passing to the high post rolling for the shot, or the corner keeping the ball for a baseline jumper. The high and low post can be interchanged and the action is run from both sides. The four-player situation involves both wings, the high post, and the low post. The wing passes and cuts. The high post rolls after he clears. The weakside wing breaks into the lane area for a pass after the post clears. Shots are developed for all four players before the action is shifted to the other side.

The 2-1-2 set utilizes guards and forwards in the two-player situations. The guard passes to the forward or low post and cuts for a return pass. Both players develop their shooting opportunities before switching to the other side. The three-player situation involves a guard, forward, and high post. The guard passes to the forward and cuts. The high post loops toward the basket for a pass and back. The shots developed are the layup off the cut maneuver, the inside move by the high post looping, and the corner jumper by the forward. The four-player situation involves both guards, the high post, and one forward or low post. The guard passes to the low post and cuts. The second guard adjusts across court to receive a pass back from the corner as in the normal pattern movement. He passes to the high post who has pivoted and backed out to the top of the key. The post passes to the guard in the corner as a result of his cut through the middle. The shooting practice includes the layup by the guard cutting, the baseline jump shot by the low post, and the baseline jump shot by the guard clearing to the corner.

The 3-2 set is employed slightly differently because of the absence of a high post. The first breakdown drill involves three players including a low post, wing, and the point. The wing passes to the low post and the point cuts through the middle for a return pass and layup. The four-player situation involves both low posts, one wing, and the point. The wing passes to the low post and the point cuts through the middle continuing to the opposite corner. The other low post loops to the basket for a pass. The shots developed are the layup down the middle, the baseline jumper, the pass inside to the low post looping for a short hook, and a pass back to the wing for a jump shot.

The 2-2-1 set utilizes a guard, wing, and low post in the breakdown drill to develop the cutter action. The guard starts the action by passing to the wing. The wing passes to the corner to the low post moving wide. The guard cuts through the middle looking for a pass from the low post. Shooting emphasis includes the layup on the cut, the baseline jumper, and a pass back to the wing for a jump shot. The four-player situation involves one guard, both wings, and the single low post. The wing passes to the low post in the corner. The guard cuts through the middle and clears. The weakside wing moves across the lane towards the ball for a pass and shot. Shots are presented through the middle via the cutter, in the corner with the low post, weakside wing moving into the lane area, and by passing back to the strongside wing for a jump shot.

Finally, the 1-3-1 overload utilizes a strongside wing and low post to isolate the cutting maneuver with two players. The strongside wing passes to the low post stepping out from his tight lane position and cuts to the basket. A return pass is given for the layup or kept for the baseline jumper by the low post. The three-player situation includes the strongside wing, the

Breakdown Drills to Develop the Multiple Set Zone Offense 105

low post, and the high post. The wing passes to the low post moving wide and cuts. The high post delays until the cutter has cleared. He then moves to the position vacated by the wing to receive a pass from the low post. Shots are developed on the cut, the corner jumper, and the pass to the high post in the wing position for a jump shot. The four player situation involves the strongside wing, weakside wing, low post, and high post. The strongside wing passes to the low post and cuts. The high post moves out to the strongside wing position. The weakside wing delays momentarily until the high post area is clear then breaks sharply to an open spot in the lane and finishing up in the high post. Shooting opportunities exist with the cutter, the high post moving to the wing position, the weakside wing breaking across the lane and the low post from his corner position.

In concluding, breakdown drills are extremely beneficial to developing team awareness. However, these drills cannot be crammed into a short period of time. They should be spread throughout the season and used accordingly when needed to re-emphasize certain available opportunities.

POST OPTIONS

The single most important element in freeing a post man to receive a pass inside the defense is timing. If a rolling maneuver is started too soon, the cutter will pratially screen the post man from receiving a pass. If the roll is late, the defense has plenty of time to adjust and cut off any effective movement. And if there is no other offensive action to camouflage the roll, the movement must be exact to have any chance of getting the ball inside the defense for a good shot. Isolating the post options through the use of breakdown drills is essential to improving player timing, team awareness, and pattern execution. All of the sets can utilize the two, three, and four man breakdown drills as mentioned in the cutter option.

The 1-3-1 set involves the high and low post in the two man situations. The low post starts with the ball in his normal wide position where he would receive the pass. He uses a verbal command or slaps the ball to initiate the roll by the high post. This helps develop the timing necessary between the high and low post to complete a pass on a roll maneuver. Shots are taken from the corner and the lane by the high post who may pull up for a jump shot or continue to the basket for a short hook shot or power layup. The three player situation involves the high post, low post, and the weakside wing. It is a continuation of the two man drill with the addition of the weakside wing breaking to an open spot after the high post clears. The same shots are developed plus the inside action created by the weakside wing breaking to an open spot in the lane. The four player breakdown drill involves the strongside wing, weakside wing, low post, and high post. The pass is initiated by the strongside wing passing to the low post moving wide to the corner. The high post rolls and clears while the weakside wing breaks into the lane area for a pass. Shots are developed with the baseline jumper, the roll inside, the weakside wing breaking into the lane, and pass back to the strongside wing for the jumper.

The 2-1-2 set utilizes a high post and a low post in the two-man drill. The low post starts with the ball in a wide position where he would normally receive the ball on a pass from the guard. A verbal command or slapping the ball starts the high post rolling for the ball. The corner jumper and the inside movement for a shot are practiced. The three-man drill incorporates the two low post players and the high post. A verbal command or slap starts the high post rolling. As he clears, the opposite low post loops to the basket for the ball and a short hook shot or power move. The four players employed in the next drill are both guards and both low post players. A guard passes into a low post moving wide. He holds his position and the opposite low post delays a three-second count to simulate the high post clearing. He then loops to the basket for a pass inside.

The 3-2 set involves both low post players in the two player situation. One low post player starts with the ball in a wide position. He proceeds to practice a head and shoulder fake, a jab step fake, or a rocker step fake. During his faking maneuvers, the other low post moves to a semi-high post position. At the conclusion of the fakes, he rolls from his position across the lane to receive a pass and continues to the basket. The feeder can also take the stationary jump shot after his series of fakes. The three-player breakdown drill involves one wing and both low posts. The wing performs a fake to bring the

Breakdown Drills to Develop the Multiple Set Zone Offense   107

opposite low post to a semi-high post position. The wing passes to the low post moving wide on his side. This keys the post roll to the basket for a pass and shot. The four-player drill includes both low posts, one wing, and the point. The point fakes and draws a low post up to a semi-high position. He passes to the wing who passes immediately to the low post on his side moving wide. The pass is made inside to the other low post rolling from his semi-high position.

In the 2-2-1 set the two-man drill is formed with a wing and the low post stationed on the opposite side. The wing starts with the ball and practices the fakes previously mentioned. During the faking maneuver, the low post moves to a semi-high post position. At the conclusion of the fakes the post rolls from his position across the lane to receive a pass and continues to the basket. The three-man situation incorporates the other wing along with the original two. The weakside wing performs the same procedure in faking as covered previously. The low post rolls to the basket from his semi-high position already assumed. After he clears, the strongside wing loops into the lane area for a pass and shot. The four-man situation includes the low post, both wings and the weakside guard. The guard passes to the weakside wing as the low post moves to a semi-high position. As the wing receives the pass, the post man rolls. As he clears, the original strongside wing loops into the lane looking for a pass and shot.

The 1-3-1 overload set initiates the two-man drill with a weakside wing tight on the lane and the high post. The wing starts with the ball and backs away on a dribble from his weakside positioning to a normal wing position. This keys the high post to roll to the basket looking for the ball. Shots are taken by the post inside with a hook or jumper. The three-man drill incorporates the point, the weakside wing, and the high post. The point starts the movement by dribbling across the top of the key towards the weakside. The wing moves wide to receive a pass. As the wing receives a pass, the high post rolls to the basket. The ball is delivered inside for a shot. The four-man situation involves the point, weakside wing, high post, and the low post. The point initiates movement by dribbling once again across the top of the key towards the weakside. The weakside moves wide to receive a pass, the high post rolls on the pass reception by the wing. After the high post rolls and clears, the low post shoots to the high post looking for quick pass inside the lane for a shot.

In concluding, there are different practice schedules to follow incorporating breakdown drills. After discussing the two, three, and four-player drills that can be developed to increase offense efficiency, overall methods are needed to insure proper utilization of the breakdown drills. The multiple set zone offense is incorporated through the whole-part-whole method, the whole being the institution of a complete individual set and all the options available in examining the pattern. The part method consists of employing breakdown drills to re-emphasize the importance of all player movement in timing and execution. The drills can be constructed in a variety of ways. One method is working on two-man passing situations in a particular practice session, three-man situations in a different practice session, and four-man situations in still another practice. This would also include segmenting cut and roll situations similarly in different sessions. A second method is employing the various two, three, and four player breakdown drills of a specific set in one practice session and likewise complete the other sets in different practices. A third method involves concentrating on the odd front sets and related breakdown drills in one session, and concentrating on the even front sets in another practice session. Still another method for variation includes emphasing the breakdown situations of all sets employing a high post operative in one practice session and emphasize those sets without a high post in a different practice. Further methods of varying the practice lineup would be dividing the sets which utilize the wing position, guard position, single low post, and double low post for concentration in different practices. By using these variations, repetition in cementing player movement along with maintaining player interest is the end result. The length of time spent in practice on the different situations will vary according to the time of the season. Early in the season time will be spent primarily on the initial learning of the complete pattern. As the season progresses more specialized emphasis is devoted on particular sets or breakdown situations depending on:

1. The upcoming opponent and their zone tendencies.
2. Weaknesses detected in scrimmages and games.

Breakdown Drills to Develop the Multiple Set Zone Offense　　109

3. Needed improvement on shooting performance.
4. Lack of ability in securing good percentage shots via the pattern.

Finally, the whole method is employed again in terms of providing adequate work in practice against the zone defenses each specific set is most effective against.

CUT AND REVERSE MANEUVER

This action was described previously as automatic in nature when mentioned with the cutter option of each set. Therefore, it is necessary to perfect this movement by isolating and incorporating it in the form of a breakdown drill. A defensive player is needed to emphasize the area where the cutter makes the proper step back. The defensive player will assume a position on the lane ball side to prevent a pass to the cutter as he nears the basket. The defender will perform with token resistance to allow the offensive player an opportunity to execute the reverse step maneuver at the conclusion of his basic cut. As the cutter reaches the basket area the defender will be between him and the ball to discourage an incoming pass. But at the same time, the cutter is in a position behind the defender to prevent him from being seen momentarily. If the defender completely ignores the cutter, this is an excellent time to perform the reverse step along the baseline towards the ball. This is done when the cutter reaches the basket and before he clears to the other side. He takes one or two steps toward the ball looking for a pass. On a reception that is close to the basket, all players are instructed to attempt a power move to the basket for the foul. Diagram 7-1 shows the position of the players and the movement pattern of the cutter in the 1-3-1 set for the reverse step action.

This opportunity will present itself generally when the deep defenders step up to high or get lazy and ignore the cutter.

REVERSING THE PASSING ACTION

As with the cut and reverse, this maneuver is created by the reaction of the defense. Therefore it is important to spend additional time perfecting this movement through concentration on the specific action. Basically the concept revolves around passing opposite the flow of the defense to produce a quick open-

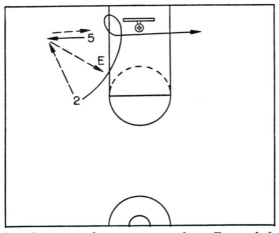

Diagram 7-1

ing for a good percentage shot. Zone defenses react as a unit to the continuous flow of the ball in a single direction. After a while the defense begins to anticipate the next pass and at times over-reacts to the ball. A simple action on the part of any offensive player is to break the single direction continuity of the ball by faking and reversing a pass back in the opposite direction. In many cases the defense will be caught out of position. The most effective way to take advantage of this concept is to implement it during the cutting option of the various sets. An example of this can be shown through the cutting action of the 3-2 set (Diagram 7-2). 1 passes to 2 on the wing. 2 passes to 4 in the corner. 1 performs his cut through the middle and out to the opposite corner. The option concludes with 4 passing back to 2. 2 passes to 3 adjusting over. 3 passes to 1 in the corner using 5 as a screen. As the continuity of the option is continued, the defense will be able to analyze the play. As the game progresses the defense be-

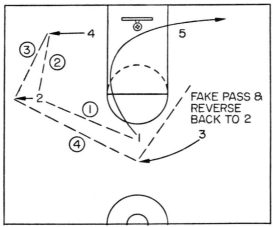

Diagram 7-2

Breakdown Drills to Develop the Multiple Set Zone Offense 111

cause of tiring or because they are aware of what will take place tend to anticipate the movement and shift prematurely to prevent the corner jump shot. Consequently the defense is taking themselves out of position should the pass be faked in the anticipated direction and reversed back. Therefore occasionally as 4 passes back to 2, 2 passes to 3, 3 fakes a pass to 1 and passes quickly back to 2 for a shot or 4 who will also be open momentarily until the defense reacts back. However, this maneuver is emphasized as the game progresses and not initially to make it more effective when the time is right.

FAKING AND PENETRATING POINTS

A third automatic maneuver which is perfected using the breakdown situation is the concept of faking and penetrating. The passing options of the sets utilize the penetration factor most effectively. The passing movement or the ball tends to spread the defense out. This permits the offensive player an opportunity to fake the next pass and penetrate between two defenders to create a good scoring possibility. An example would be creating a two on one using the 2-2-1 set against a 1-3-1 zone. Offensive players 1 and 3 have a two on one passing situation advantage against defender B or 2 and 4 against D. Player 1 is splitting defenders A-B with 3 splitting B-E. Player 2 is splitting defenders A-D and 4 splitting D-E. (Diagram 7-3.)

Since the multiple set zone offense is based on committing and gapping the defense, this maneuver when presented falls in complete agreement with the offensive theory and can be ex-

Diagram 7-3

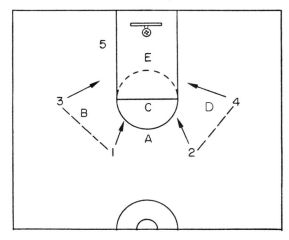

112   *Breakdown Drills to Develop the Multiple Set Zone Offense*

tremely effective. Formal practice on this is conducted on the basis of organizing offensive advantages in the ratio of 2 on 1, 3 on 2, and 4 on 3 from the set formations opposing different zone defenses.

SUMMARY

Breakdown drills are an integral part of installing any offensive system. They are necessary to improve timing, execution, and knowledge. In instituting the multiple set system there are ten steps to use as guidelines.

1. Diagram and explain the entire offense on the blackboard and show the basic movement pattern.
2. Place the players in their proper distribution on the floor and walk them through the offensive options.
3. All players are then divided into units to perform the movement at one basket. This allows the unit on the floor to learn through movement and the units off the floor through visual analysis.
4. After the basic groundwork of the system is laid, two baskets are used as the players run through the offense concurrently and minor corrections on positioning and angles in reference to passing are made.
5. The players return to one basket and perform the offense with a defense offering token resistance — moving with the ball but not attempting to steal or deflect passes.
6. Utilizing a half-court scrimmage situation and giving the offensive team five opportunities. Corrections are made immediately when mistakes occur.
7. After the basic concepts are across, breakdown drills are then instituted as outlined for improving timing and execution.
8. The sets are then examined in operation against the various zone defenses which they will oppose.
9. Re-emphasizing the timing factor necessary and correcting the weaknesses noted.
10. Utilizing the total set concept in scrimmage variations at both half and full court.

CHAPTER EIGHT

Offensive Strategy of the Multiple Set Zone Offense

Offensive strategy is defined as the attempt to create scoring opportunities by utilizing specific patterns designed to get the job done. This will be dictated by the defense of the opposition and the specific individual abilities of team members. There are basic principles and methods developed through experience and research which when properly utilized will produce sound offensive thrust. This includes both an individual approach to specific defenses as well as a general offensive philosophy, which together form the basis for offensive strategy.

PLAYING FOR CLOSE SHOTS

There is no set number of passes that must be completed against a zone defense before a shot is taken in any offensive pattern. However, through experience it has been found that patience on offense cannot be overemphasized in gaining a good scoring opportunity. The terminology of close-in reference to securing a shot does not specifically mean an exact distance from the basket. It means moving to a position where the best

114 *Offensive Strategy of the Multiple Set Zone Offense*

possible shot will occur under the circumstances. An example will explain this concept. In one particular season our front line starters were 6' 4", 6' 2", and 6' 2". We were opposing a team using a front line of 6' 9", 6' 8", and 6' 4". They defensed us with a box and 1 on our best player, who was a guard. We utilized our 1-3-1 set to split the defensive positioning. Our players were instructed to penetrate the first line of defense and be satisfied with the 8-12' jump shots rather than attempting to drive on the size of their big men. With this in mind the players had a great deal of confidence in their shooting responsibility and we were fortunate to win the game 51-50. In this instance the close shot was defined by the size of the opponents. In other situations with a smaller team, the close shot would be nearer to the basket.

Regardless of the approach to shooting, there are basic rules in obtaining close shots.

1. Each player must hustle to his position to exhibit a strong offensive appearance.
2. Communication is essential so each player knows exactly which option is being run.
3. Execution of the pattern is necessary to generate offensive opportunities.
4. Confidence in the scoring attempt as defined by the close shot theory is a must.
5. Patience in securing the shot in the range desired is always in effect.
6. Repetition in practice concerning the area of shooting responsibility for any particular game is needed.

PERCENTAGE SHOOTING

The topic of percentage shooting is extremely important but oftentimes misunderstood or mistaken for shooting percentage. This concept does not refer to the percentage tabulated by dividing the number shots taken into the number of shots made. Specifically this is the shooting percentage. Percentage shooting refers to the selection of a shot based on the factors of type of shot taken, position the shot is taken from, individual ability of the player, body balance, and positioning of the rest of the team. It is important to instill in each player his responsibility to the team to take only those shots which have the greatest

Offensive Strategy of the Multiple Set Zone Offense 115

chance of being made, and allowing the team an opportunity for a second effort if it does not.

Some examples of poor percentage shooting situations include:

1. A guard driving to the basket in heavy congestion and veering out towards the corner and attempting a hook shot.
2. A post man being overplayed and forced to the top of the key to receive the pass, turning and taking a 20' jump shot.
3. Players getting trapped in the corner without a passing lane open and shooting the ball simply to get rid of it before being tied up.
4. A player in a fast break situation is stopped from penetrating, and shoots an 18' jump shot because nobody else is around to pass to.
5. A player on an offensive rebound jumping almost backwards to get the shot off against much taller opposition.

Oftentimes players are not aware of what a good percentage shot is and that there are variations depending on individual ability. Percentage shooting is not a general concept to treat everyone alike. Each player possesses a unique shooting ability and it must be used to advantage in the best way possible to benefit the team. Statistics play a vital role in analyzing individual differences in shooting ability. In our system we use three methods in revealing shooting trends of players.

1. Each player is required to shoot a specific number of shots from five basic spots on the perimeter and record them daily on mimeographed charts. The spots are 15-18' from the basket located in the right corner, left corner, left wing at a forty-five degree angle on the foul line extended, right wing at a forty-five degree angle on the foul line extended, and from one step inside the top of the key. Each spot is recorded daily to show individual improvement and the best percentage shooting spot for each player. An additional advantage in recording shooting totals is that the player will concentrate more than he normally would during

116   *Offensive Strategy of the Multiple Set Zone Offense*

a free shooting period. These shooting statistics can be extremely important, particularly when mapping the game plan against zone defenses. Some individuals are pure shooters and can be used as such against zone defenses when the basic need is to put the ball in the basket.

2. Charting shots during half court and full court scrimmage sessions can reveal three shooting tendencies. In the first place the best percentage spots for players can be checked. Second, shooting preferences of players in relation to particular areas on the floor can be analyzed. And third, the reaction of players under stressful shooting conditions can be noted. Certain players respond better under stress than others.

3. Charting actual games is a followup and a continuation to the practice charts, with the pressure of the game becoming an additional factor in determining the best percentage shooters.

Statistics not only reveal percentage shooting but also aid in preparing offensive strategy by making minor adjustments:

1. Switching a player from one wing position to the other wing because his individual statistics have shown that he shoots better from one particular side of the floor.

2. Switching players to accommodate the offensive movement. Players will shoot better moving in one direction in certain instances.

3. Determining the player who will take the last second shot in a game and approximately where he should attempt to take it from. The opposing team will normally expect the ball to go to the leading scorer. However, he is probably not the best percentage shooter on the team. In which case the ball should be given to the player who has exhibited the best percentage shooting record. It may be the second, third, fourth, or even the fifth scorer on the team. To increase the chances of making the shot, the player designated should attempt to set up in his best shooting area predetermined by his shooting records.

4. Selecting the offensive set to take advantage of an individual who shoots extremely well from a specific position on the floor.

There are two different philosophies in effect in terms of field goal shooting. On one hand some coaches feel the more shots taken will result in more shots made. On the other hand some coaches adopt the theory of percentage shooting. We operate under the latter concept and have achieved success with it. In the past five seasons our team has averaged only 57 shots per game. During that period the overall team shooting percentage has been 41.9%. The result has been a winning percentage of 70%. Percentage shooting has two great advantages. In the first place it applies a great deal of pressure on the defense knowing the ball will not be given up easily. Second, the opponent also has offensive pressure knowing they must score to prevent us from controlling the tempo of the game.

ATTACKING THE WEAK AREAS OF ZONES

Each zone defense has specific area weaknesses which are inherent in its makeup. The weak areas are primarily defined by the absence of defensive players. The advantage of using the multiple set zone offense is that weaknesses of all zones can be exploited by employing specific sets to concentrate on the weak areas. Diagram 8-1 shows the major weak spots of the 3-2 and 1-2-2 zones.

The offensive sets used to operate against the weak areas include the 1-3-1 set, 2-1-2 set, 2-2-1 set, and 1-3-1 overload. Specifically the 1-3-1 set utilizes the high post extremely well

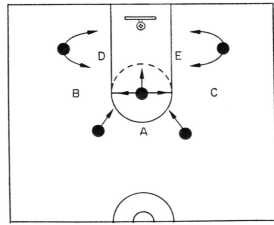

along with movement from the wing position to the corner. The 2-1-2 set works the high post area and the area between defenders A-B and A-C to penetrate for 15'-18' jump shots. The 2-2-1 set operates on the area between defenders A-B and A-C. When the wing defenders B or C move up to discourage the penetration, the offensive wing 3 or 4 drops behind the defender and looks for a drop pass from the guard. The 1-3-1 overload takes advantage of good outside shooting from the wing position. If the defensive wings play between the point and the strongside to discourage a pass, two possibilities exist. The first move is to pass inside to the high post who has been left unguarded, or the strongside wing moves down to the corner to receive a lob pass from the point for a shot.

The major difference between a 3-2 and 1-2-2 zone is the width of the wing defenders. In the 1-2-2 the wing defenders B and C assume a tighter position on the lane. It protects the middle better than the 3-2 but allows more operating room around the perimeter of the zone. The same sets utilized to attack the 3-2 zone are used against the 1-2-2. However, since the middle is protected better, more movement is directed to the wing and corner positions.

Diagram 8-2 shows the major weak spots of the 1-3-1 zone.

The sets designed to take advantage of the characteristic weak areas are the 2-1-2 and 2-2-1 sets. The 2-1-2 splits defenders A and B, A and D. When the defensive wing moves up to stop penetration, the guard passes off to the low post on his side moving wide to the corner. The 2-2-1 also takes advantage of the area between A-B and A-D. The offensive

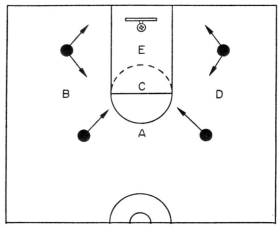

Diagram 8-2

Offensive Strategy of the Multiple Set Zone Offense 119

wings hold their position until the defensive wings commit themselves and then drop behind or wide to receive a pass. A variation is to place the wing man on the side of the low post outside the defensive wing, and the other wing man inside the defensive wing in his area. This provides inside help and prevents the defense from overshifting.

Diagram 8-3 shows the weak spots of the 2-1-2 and 2-3 zones.

Diagram 8-3

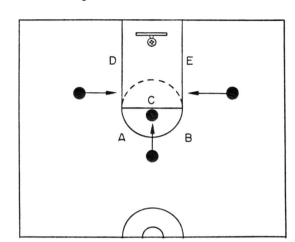

The 1-3-1 set, 1-3-1 overload set, and 3-2 set can be used effectively against these zones. The 1-3-1 is the ideal set because it allows penetration between defenders A-B as well as movement from the wing positions. The 1-3-1 overload primarily works on the wing position as determined by the strongside designation. The 3-2 set operates on the point area and also the wing area. However, without a post man freezing the middle defender C it is difficult to penetrate down the middle.

A zone defense very seldom seen is the 2-2-1 zone. But the possibility does exist and therefore should be considered. Diagram 8-4 shows the weak areas of the 2-2-1 zone.

As in the other even front zones, the 1-3-1, 3-2, and 1-3-1 overload sets are utilized. When employing these sets against the 2-2-1, the wing men move deeper to exploit the weakness in the corner position. Of course the absence of a middle defender makes the high post a prime target.

In summarizing briefly on the method of attacking the weak

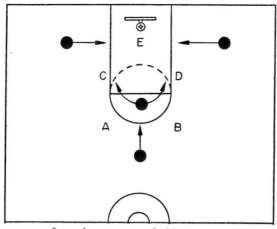

Diagram 8-4

areas of various zone defenses, two important principles are in operation. First of all the front line zone defensive players determine the initial offensive alignment. Even front zones (2-1-2, 2-3, 2-2-1) are attacked with an odd front set (3-2, 1-3-1, 1-3-1 overload). Odd front zone defenses (3-2, 1-2-1, 1-3-1) are attacked with an even front set (2-1-2, 2-2-1). Secondly, after the basic defensive alignment is established, the offensive concentration is in the weak areas of the specific zone being confronted with. In the multiple set offensive system there are two odd front sets (1-3-1, 3-2), two even front sets (2-1-2, 2-2-1), and one overload set (1-3-1). This allows a minimum of three offensive sets to attack specific zone defenses under the even-odd concept. Through experience, I have found that the 1-3-1 overload set can be effective against all zone defenses with minor adjustments being made in certain situations. It becomes particularly effective when a player is experiencing a hot shooting hand from either wing position. It is simply a matter of shifting the overload to the side which he is scoring from. The overload also takes advantage of a player whose individual strength is receiving the ball in the high post and turning immediately for the fifteen foot jump shot. The next phase after selecting the proper set is to systematically incorporate the options available in the pattern. Perimeter passing is the first option of the offense to operate and test the defensive movement. Rapid passing will determine if the defense is aggressive, sagging to close off the middle, overshifting on particular players, or attempting to trap the ball on the sideline or in the corner. The defensive reaction to the ball movement will then dictate whether

Offensive Strategy of the Multiple Set Zone Offense **121**

or not to continue with the straight passing option to secure scoring opportunities. Failure to penetrate the defense for good percentage shots is the deciding factor to employ the cut and roll options of the pattern to create more player movement.

CONTROLLING THE TEMPO OF THE GAME

There are basic factors to consider when this aspect of offensive strategy is discussed.

1. A breather is caught on offense, not on defense. A great deal of energy is expended on defense when the attempt is to get the ball and prevent the opponent from scoring.
2. A team cannot score without the ball. Therefore, the team on offense is in control.
3. Teams that play primarily a zone defense generally do not exert a lot of effort on defense. They will work aggressively on the first and second pass, but will have a tendency to settle back and encourage the shot in an attempt to get the ball back.
4. Teams that zone 100% of the time are usually fast break conscious and will commit errors on defense because of their intense desire to get the ball and score.
5. The number of shots taken is not the most important offensive consideration, the number of good percentage shots is.

Some coaches feel the more shots taken will result in more points scored. This may be true, but by the same token the opponent is also allowed more opportunities to score. Controlling the ball essentially means to execute the offensive patterns until a good percentage shooting situation presents itself. This may occur after one pass or ten passes. There is no set number of passes which must be completed before a shot is taken. It is sound offensive theory to work until a good opportunity exists. There is no difference if the final score is 81 to 80 or 41 to 40. The record is still the same in the won-loss column.

Offensive control dictates the tempo of the game. It can drive a zone team into a man for man defense in an attempt to get

122   *Offensive Strategy of the Multiple Set Zone Offense*

the ball. This forced change can produce a tremendous advantage. Some teams are so concerned with offensive averages and team scoring output they may have a tendency to rush their shots in an attempt to score quickly. Controlling the ball on offense minimizes the number of fouls committed on defense. This alone can save valuable fouls which may be needed in the later stages of a game to gain possession of the ball. It can also increase the number of fouls committed by the opponent in their efforts to get the ball. This can result in a 1-1 situation going into effect early in the game.

PATIENCE ON OFFENSE

As mentioned before, there are teams employing a zone defense because they are primarily offensive minded. These teams are willing to trade shot for shot and hope the ball will be given up quickly. This in turn increases the tempo of the game and allows the opponent to initiate the fast break more often. However, the offensive minded team will not generally sustain a good defensive thrust. In most cases the team will remain aggressive on the first couple of passes to steal the ball, or give the impression that a better shot cannot be obtained. Patience will cause the defense to settle back, opening up better and closer opportunities. Constant movement of the ball will tire the defense. Patient play develops team attitude as all five players are working as a unit to secure good shots. Pressure is relieved from any one player being responsible for all of the scoring.

MAINTAINING FLOOR BALANCE

It is essential in any offensive system of play that proper floor balance be maintained at all times. This indicates that a team is always ready to react both offensively and defensively as situations develop. Offensive floor balance is important so that each player is aware of his four teammates on the floor along with the responsibilities of their individual positions. This is necessary for pattern execution and preventing additional pressure tactics by the defense. Floor balance also enables the offense more opportunity to penetrate the defense. Other important considerations include designating primary and secondary rebounders, providing a defensive safety against the fast

Offensive Strategy of the Multiple Set Zone Offense 123

break, and most importantly floor balance gives confidence to the players because they know where they are supposed to be. Proper team attitude is an item definitely improved by maintaining floor balance. It eliminates excuse-making such as "I thought that was his responsibility," "He was supposed to be there."

REACTING QUICKLY FROM OFFENSE TO DEFENSE

It is a basic assumption that any team to be consistently successful must be able to make a good transition from offense to defense. If a team shoots 40% from the field, 60% of the shots are available for the opponent to secure rebounds and initiate fast break opportunities. A good transition relieves a lot of additional pressure at the offensive end of the court. Patterns can be run and shots taken confidently knowing that a missed shot will not result in an easy fast break layup for the opponent. Every player has specific responsibilities as dictated by the coach and situations that develop. Responsibilities will change and each player must be constantly aware of his own. On every shot there are three primary rebounders, one primary defender as a safety valve, and the fifth player who doubles as a secondary rebounder or secondary defender depending upon his position on the floor.

OVERSHIFTING THE DEFENSE

All zone defenses start from a basic formation of players determined by the type used. As the ball is moved, the zone defense moves as a unit to cover. By using a perimeter passing formation the defensive shifting of each zone can be analyzed. At times the defense will overshift because of anxiousness, aggressiveness, or anticipation. Emphasis on the passing option available will diagnose in what position and situation on the floor that the defense has a tendency to overshift. This knowledge is valuable in developing offensive pressure by specializing in the techniques of splitting the defense, working passing triangles, reversing the pass, and penetrating the defense. Teams that overshift in the zone generally attempt to trap. The logical passes to cut off are from the wing to point, wing to high post, and corner to corner. After analyzing what passing situations the defense has a tendency to overshift on, avoiding the vulnerable

124 *Offensive Strategy of the Multiple Set Zone Offense*

passing lanes will eliminate trapping possibilities by the defense and decrease the probability of having a pass intercepted.

REMAINING ACTIVE ON OFFENSE

An active offense is necessary against zone defenses to remain competitive. Nothing hurts offensive possibilities more than when a player or the ball remains stationary for any length of time. This allows the defense an opportunity to rest and regain energy to deny passing lanes by applying additional pressure. Inactivity also places a great deal of pressure and causes anxiety with the rest of the players who are waiting to see what develops. Momentarily the offense will be stationary until the pattern begins to unfold with the selection of the proper option. However, once the offense is in motion the defense must likewise react and move. There are five choices which the offensive player has at his disposal when he receives a pass. His first thought should be to face the basket for a shot if he is in a good percentage position. Second, the player looks to deliver a pass to any cutter moving through the defense. Third, if the defense has overshifted in anticipation he quickly reverses the ball back to catch the defense off guard in hopes of opening up a good shooting possibility. The fourth choice consists of faking an overaggressive defender out of position and penetrating on a dribble for a shot or pass off inside. And the fifth choice available consists of passing the ball and cutting to the basket. All of these choices are determined instantaneously by the reaction of the defense to the ball. They are not pre-determined by the player before he receives the ball. Constant repetition in theory and practice correction is needed to perfect these techniques.

EMPHASIZING OFFENSE EFFICIENCY

The area of offensive efficiency cannot be over-emphasized in developing an offensive attack capable of pressuring the defense. We stress the importance of offense efficiency by using two specialized charts which aid us in determining how efficient our offensive attempts are. In analyzing our past games a statistic turned up which we felt could be extremely valuable in showing the players the importance of establishing a consistent offensive thrust. The statistics alerted us to the fact that

Offensive Strategy of the Multiple Set Zone Offense 125

if we averaged one point every time we had possession of the ball or scored one basket every two times down the floor, the winning percentage would have been 95%. The one point average figure is realistic and the players become increasingly aware of the importance of effective ball possession.

The second chart designed for offense efficiency is based on the number of lost possessions without a shooting attempt. Lost possessions are grouped into two categories specifically termed turnovers and give-a-ways, the significant difference being that turnovers are classified as lost possessions via offensive fouls, violations or any situation in which the ball becomes dead immediately. This will at least allow the offensive team to recover on defense without giving up a fast break layup. On the other hand, give-a-ways are classified as lost possessions while the ball remains alive. These would include having the ball stolen, throwing a bad pass, and any other situation in which the ball is lost to the opponent and an immediate score may result.

At the conclusion of each game the lost possession totals are analyzed in terms of the score at the time the ball was lost and whether or not the opponent converted the opportunity into a direct score. The value of this knowledge re-emphasizes to the players the necessity of maintaining possession of the ball and not giving it up without generating a scoring attempt. Complete elimination of turnovers or give-a-ways will never occur. The objective is to minimize the number that are created and be able to show the players in black and white the results that can occur in determining wins and losses.

CHAPTER NINE

Multiple Set Option Selection Against Situation Zones

As covered in Chapter Eight concerning the individual sets which comprise the multiple set zone offense, certain sets are more effective against specific zone defenses. Within the boundaries of the different zone defenses there are specific situations which can be developed. Therefore, the next area of prime consideration concerns the implementing of particular offensive movement to counteract any type of variation employed by the defense. A defensive adjustment regardless of how minor oftentimes can confuse the offensive pattern or throw the offense off stride by imposing specifically designed tactics. Depending on the type of and position of the defensive pressure, the offensive objective is to keep the ball away from the areas on the floor that would make it advantageous for the defense.

ATTACKING THE CORNER TRAP

The corner trap is a much-used technique when employing a zone defense. Generally the 1-3-1, 1-2-2, and 3-2 zone defenses use this defensive tactic most often because of the basic defensive positioning used in organizing these zones. The corner trap operates in either of two ways. When the ball is passed into the corner, the defensive forward moves out for coverage. The defensive wing shuts the sideline passing lane off and moves into the corner to complete the trap maneuver for an attempted steal or possible jump ball. The second method is for the defensive wing man following the dribbler into the corner and the defensive forward quickly moving out to complete the trap. In both cases available passing lanes are cut off by defensive overplays. The defensive point moves over to cover the pass back outside. The other wing moves into the lane to prevent a pass inside to the post. The other defensive forward moves across the lane to prevent a pass underneath.

In attacking the corner trap setup there are certain offensive adjustments necessary and are based on the following guidelines:

1. Eliminate all dribbling into a corner position.
2. Eliminate passing into the corner except as a last resort or as a possible outlet pass to prevent a steal out front.
3. Due to the nature of the defensive pressure through an overshifting of players, a set incorporating a high post (1-3-1, 2-1-2, 1-3-1 overload) enables an additional passing alternative to relieve pressure.
4. The anticipation factor makes it necessary to emphasize the passing option initially to force the defense out of position and provide possible penetration lanes.

In consideration of the above factors, the cut options in the various sets would be virtually eliminated when opposing the corner trap zone since all offensive cuts originate with a pass into the corner. The 3-2 set and 2-2-1 set would not be used because player placement dictates that the defense is playing five on three when flooding one side to force the trap in the corner. Therefore, the 1-3-1, 2-1-2, and 1-3-1 overload sets would be the most effective patterns against the trap. These sets allow the offense to open up the attack, make available more passing lanes, and allow weakside action by hitting the high post after the defense has overshifted. The passing and roll options prove most effective against the trap because they tend to spread out

Multiple Set Option Selection Against Situation Zones 129

the defense and still produce offensive openings to secure good percentage shooting situations.

DEFEATING MIDCOURT PRESSURE

Midcourt pressure is a defensive maneuver that generally occurs in the form of a half-court trap press. Defenses may stay with the pressure, fall back into a zone after initial penetration by the offense, or fall back into a straight zone after a pre-designated number of passes. The reasons for employing this form of defensive pressure are:

1. Extremely quick guards that are capable of deflecting and intercepting passes.
2. A short and narrow court which cuts down the movement area for the defense to pressure.
3. The offensive guards cannot handle pressure.
4. A short team attempting to prevent the ball as much as possible from being passed inside.

In setting up and attacking this defensive form it is necessary to determine whether the front line defense is even or odd and if the backline defense has a middle man. The offensive formation is predicated on the defensive alignment in utilizing the even-odd attacking principle. Second, a determination of the type of pressure must be analyzed. It might be direct pressure on the ball in a 1 on 1 situation, in which case the proper reaction is to avoid dribbling into an eventual double team by passing to a forward breaking up to the top of the key behind the front line defense.

The pressure might develop by forcing the ball to the side and follow up with a trap using the sideline to advantage. In this case the ball should never be passed directly from back court to a corner position in front court. This is a very delicate pass to attempt and must be extremely accurate to hit the target. Second, passing lanes are cut off and greater defensive pressure is allowed to develop.

The proper maneuver is to advance the ball up the middle of the court against even front pressure to draw the defense in for a commitment before dropping the ball off to a wing in the area vacated by the defensive guard applying pressure. Diagram 9-1

130   *Multiple Set Option Selection Against Situation Zones*

Diagram 9-1

Diagram 9-2

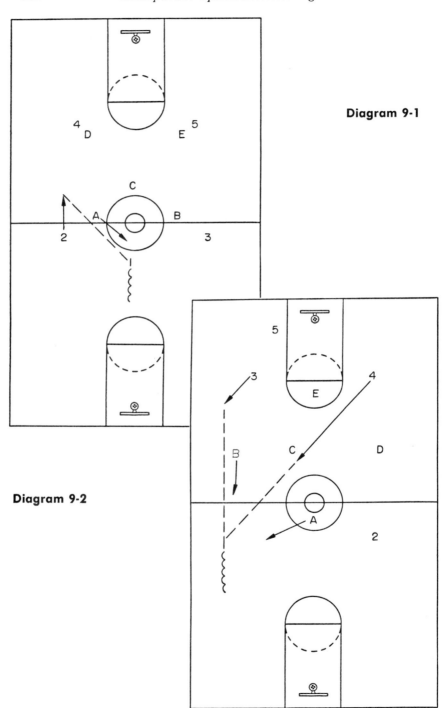

Multiple Set Option Selection Against Situation Zones 131

shows this technique. Against an odd front press the ball is brought up the side to bring the defensive point to the ball. The next pass against either form of defensive pressure is to an active forward moving beyond the front line defense either to the middle or sideline for an opening. Diagram 9-2 illustrates this technique.

The third kind of midcourt pressure involves allowing the first pass in front court and then moving into a double team or trap situation. It is important that the offensive players realize what is developing and not to pass the ball into an automatic trap area. These would include the corners and the area bounded by the time line and sideline. There are specific offensive options which become available and can be very effective.

As the ball is received in front court, the offensive player immediately watches the defensive reaction without dribbling. If a second defensive player moves into the area, a pass is made to a player in the direction from which the second defensive player came. The offensive players remain in a wide spread formation and utilize a high post to create additional passing lanes. Diagram 9-3 shows the direction of the pass on a specific trap maneuver.

Generally midcourt pressure in the form of a trap is a temporary form of defense. Defenses have a tendency to fall back into their basic zone when the ball is not stolen or thrown away immediately, resulting in easy baskets. Nothing makes a press more aggressive than scoring quickly by intercepting panic passes. The important points to remember on offense are keeping team poise, spreading out the defenders, and moving the ball with quick short passes to discourage the defense from pressuring. This would include utilizing the passing options to discourage the defense by forcing them to fall back because of failure to develop an immediate double team advantage.

OPENING THE MIDDLE SAG

Closing the middle is a defensive concept used mainly by zone defenses employing a middle defender. This would include primarily the 1-3-1, 2-1-2, and 2-3 zone defenses. The defensive principle is to close off the lane area to offensive penetration either on a dribble or via a pass. It affords excellent rebounding

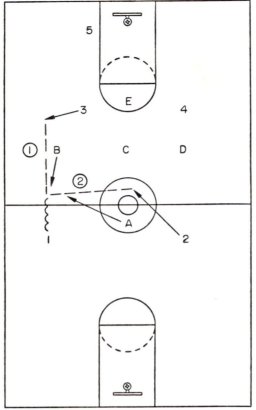

Diagram 9-3

position. Both extremes of player sizes utilize this particular form of defense. A small team will compensate for their lack of physical size by screening out and remaining close in the middle to prevent the opponent from securing second efforts. A tall team can utilize this to completely discourage any penetration and gain great rebounding advantage to initiate the fast break. Generally, by closing off the lane area, the perimeter of the zone is open to attack.

In defeating this type of defense three important points must be covered. Outside shooting is a primary means of scoring initially. The ball must be moved quickly and accurately. Patience is the key to success against this defense. Teams employing this type of zone generally have acquired a bad habit of reacting slowly. They are geared to maintain their basic distribution at all times and are primarily position conscious.

In analyzing the options to use in defeating the middle sag, certain limitations must be realized. The nature of the defense will prevent the roll option from functioning effectively because

Multiple Set Option Selection Against Situation Zones 133

of the congestion in the lane area. It will also prevent the initial man through on the cut maneuvers. However, the second and third players available on the cut can be effective by picking their spot to break to in an attempt to split the defense.

This is also an excellent situation to operate the cut and reverse maneuver and the reverse the pass action. The ability of the outside players to penetrate the front line defense forcing the back line defense to make a commitment can be very effective. This either results in a good percentage jump shot or an opportunity to pass off, as the back line defense must react up to stop the penetration.

PREVENTING PASSING LANE DENIAL

Some zone defenses attack with the principle of defensing obvious passing lanes. In doing so the defense hopes to delay movement of the ball and consequently upset the timing factor so necessary in offensive play. This will also have a tendency to deter the offensive thrust. Poise and patience are necessary ingredients to defeat this type of zone.

Under normal conditions the offense approaches this defense with the even-odd principle to form the basic groundwork. The defensive players will be positioned such as they are, splitting the offense and already obstructing passing lanes. Therefore, initially the passing option will be ineffective because the ball cannot be moved quickly enough around the perimeter of the defense. It then becomes necessary to incorporate primarily player movement without the ball as in the cut and roll options.

Second, the player with the ball can attempt penetration while the defense is spread and concerned with denying the passes to the players moving through. An example of this would be a 1-3-1 zone against the 2-1-2 set. Instead of forcing the cutter option because of the defense anticipating the passing lanes, the offense should concentrate on penetrating between two defenders for a good shot, draw the defense in, or pass off underneath. Diagram 9-4 shows this action.

RELIEVING FRONTING PRESSURE ON THE HIGH POST

The single most effective player generating offensive opportunities is the high post. He enjoys the most available pass-

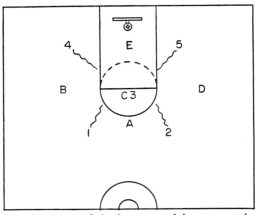

Diagram 9-4

ing lanes and is in a position to gain an excellent percentage shot from fifteen feet at the foul line. Consequently zone defenses must combat and take away these opportunities from the high post. The most effective method of accomplishing this is to prevent the post from receiving the ball as much as possible. Zone defenses with an even front generally have a middle man assigned to contest a high post player. He attempts to deny the reception by playing on the side with an arm in front to deflect incoming passes. He moves from side to side as the ball moves around the perimeter. Odd front zones will generally drop the point man back to stay in front of the high post preventing the pass in.

In the case of a 1-3-1 zone the middle man is already assigned to the high post. The nature of this defensive pressure forces the offensive players to remain active and move towards the basket. A roll option is extremely effective and if the back line defense does not react properly, a shot inside the lane area is the end result. Should the middle defender continue with the high post clearing the lane, the second man moving through the defense to the open spot in the lane will be open. Second, the cutter option will be open because he forces the low defenders to key on his movement to the basket. The high post can then roll after the cutter clears to produce another shooting opportunity. By moving the high post, pressure is applied to the defense to prevent him from being fronted and relieved of his effectiveness potency.

RELIEVING FRONTING PRESSURE ON THE LOW POST

Fronting the low post is a defensive tactic to force the low post to move higher or wider than he normally would to receive a pass. This can have a tendency to disrupt the continuity of the offensive pattern. It is important to use a high post to prevent the defense from closing off all inside passing lanes. Second, a single low post can maneuver much more effectively and easier to an open spot behind the defense. Third, the movement of offensive players is essential to make the defense work and guess where the next offensive movement is going to appear.

Moving the low post wide to initiate a cut or roll maneuver forces the low defender to make a quick decision on coverage responsibility. He also must be tremendously quick to anticipate the offensive movement of a player who is playing behind him. An active offense will produce good percentage shots without disrupting team continuity. Consequently the 1-3-1 overload and the 1-3-1 set are primarily utilized against a zone defense applying this type of defensive pressure.

DEFEATING THE MATCHUP ZONE

The matchup zone defense is a defensive variation of the straight zone defenses available. It is characterized by the defense assuming the same player setup as the offensive pattern. The reaction of the defense is based on both zone and man-for-man principles. The defense attempts to confuse the offensive pattern by utilizing such things as a 1 to 1 guarding ratio, automatic switching, fronting the post man, closing off the lane area to dribbling penetration, preventing cutters from taking good angles to the basket, and gaining excellent rebounding position for advantage. The two most popular and effective matchup zone defenses originate from a 1-2-2 and 2-3 or 2-1-2 defensive set. From these sets the defense rotates to align with the offensive formation.

In attacking this type of defense with the multiple set zone offense three offensive principles are used as guidelines. Lateral passing from guard to guard is eliminated except as a relief measure when other passing lanes are cut off. This prevents the defense from standing and automatically switching if the guards weave or cross. The passing lanes recommended are guard to wing, guard to forward, and guard to high post. These are penetration passes designed to apply pressure to the defense.

Second, stationary passing is kept to a minimum. The cut and roll options are used to take advantage of player movement, offensive penetration, and applying pressure on the defense to react. The matchup defense involves total player movement to be effective, anticipation, and proper decision-making to cut off the cutters and close off the lane area to post activity. Offensively the players must move without the ball to force the defense and execute the complete option to secure openings.

Third, it is extremely important that each set in operation must have player movement prior to initiating the actual option. This would include the low post moving to a high post position, low post moving to a wing position, wing moving to a low post position, or high post moving to a low or different high post position on the foul line. Inside movement will change defensive guarding assignments and have a tendency to occupy the defense prior to the execution of the option. At times the preliminary movement will open a player for a quick pass before the defense reacts.

There are two methods to organize the desired set. The first is to line up independently in the set formation that has been selected to combat the matchup zone. The second involves automatically lining up in the 3-2 formation each time down the floor and then with player movement rotating to the set desired. The latter method is the one utilized most often against a matchup zone. It allows the offense movement as well as concealing the eventual set alignment.

By setting up in the 3-2 formation the defense will match up likewise in a 3-2 or 1-2-2. By shooting a low post player (either 4 or 5) to a high post position on the foul line the 1-3-1 set is formed. 1 looks immediately to the high post. As 4 makes the reception he looks to the wing man on his side swinging behind the defense. High school players schooled in playing a defense with zone principles tend to follow the movement of the ball at all times. This momentary response will be enough to allow the wing man to free himself for a pass and shot. Diagram 9-5 shows the initial movement from the 3-2 formation with a low post breaking to a high post position against a matchup zone to form the 1-3-1.

As 4 receives the ball he turns immediately to face the basket. If D follows him to the high post, the weakside wing will be

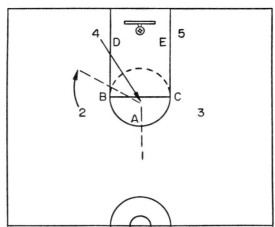

Diagram 9-5

open. If D stays low and doesn't react up with 4, a fifteen foot jump shot is the result. When both opportunities are sealed off, 4 looks to the strongside wing (3). 3 passes to 5 initiating a cut or roll by cutting through the defense or holding his position as would be the normal procedure in the cut and roll options. From the 3-2 all other sets can be formed. The 2-2-1 set is moved into by a pass from the point (1) to a wing (2). 2 looks for the opposite low post flashing into the lane and out. 2 dribbles towards the top of the key. The players rotate as 1 and 2 become the guards, 3 and 4 the wing men and 5 the single low post. (Diagram 9-6.)

The 2-1-2 set is organized from the basic 3-2 formation also by utilizing the movement of a low post moving to a high post position. The wing same side drops to a forward or low post position and the point and strongside wing rotate to become the guards in the set. (Diagram 9-7.)

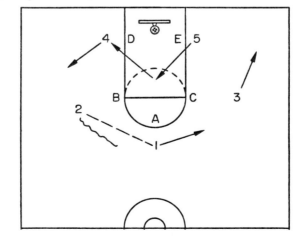

Diagram 9-6

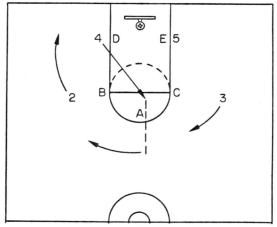

Diagram 9-7

1 attempts to hit the high post for a turn-around jump shot or pass to the weakside wing (2) dropping behind his defender. If 2 receives a pass and cannot maneuver for a short jumper, the guard (1) cuts through to initiate the cutter option. The 1-3-1 overload set is developed from the 3-2 formation by either wing man dribbling towards the baseline. If the defender in his area does not follow, he moves in for a jump shot or pass inside to the low post if the low defender moves out to stop further penetration. (Diagram 9-8.)

If defender B stays with 2, 5 breaks from his low post position across the lane to a side high post to form the overload strongside left. 2 passes into 5, who looks for the quick turn around jumper or 3 breaking behind the defense on the weakside.

The selection of sets to be used against matchup zones are determined by:

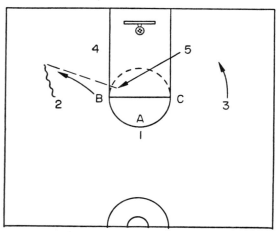

Diagram 9-8

Multiple Set Option Selection Against Situation Zones 139

1. Scouting reports on weaknesses involving players or areas.
2. Observations of defensive tendencies and automatics that the opponent employs.
3. The basic alignment of the defense each time down the floor.
4. Offensive probing early in the game to determine which sets will be most effective.

ATTACKING THE BACKLINE ZONE

A defensive variation of the matchup zone is a defensive set-up employing the backline or forwards and center in a zone and the front line or guards maintaining a man-for-man defense. It is a technique designed to confuse the offensive patterns by having the players divided in their analysis and approach to the specific defense being used.

Generally the defense will take the appearance of a 2-1-2, 2-3, or 2-2-1 formation. Certain things must be avoided when attacking this defensive form. The guards must not waste time and energy passing the ball back and forth. Second, the guards must eliminate weaving or screening to avoid a double team situation from developing. And third, the guards must avoid dribbling as a defensive player will remain with him in a normal man for man pickup. This consumes a lot of valuable time which should be devoted to moving towards the basket in penetrating.

On the positive side the guards must immediately look for a penetration pass beyond the first line of defense to the forwards and center. In attacking this defense the 3-2 formation is set up each time down the floor as against the matchup zone. This gives the point player more available passing lanes in addition to splitting the even front defense. The defense is then forced to adjust their man-for-man assignment on the front line.

Many teams encountering this may adjust by moving A and B wide to cover the wing players and moving C up to cover the point from the basic 2-1-2 formation. (Diagram 9-9.)

By doing so the defense weakens their middle defense previously occupied by C and allowing a low post (4 or 5) to break into the high post area vacated by C. 1 passes to 5. 5 turns and looks for the fifteen foot jumper. 5 next looks for 3 going back

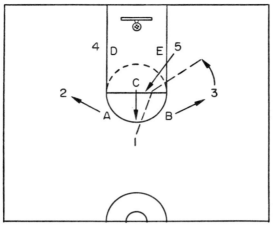

Diagram 9-9

door behind defender B. If neither opportunity is open, the offense remains in the 1-3-1 set and continues offensive movement using either the cut or roll option. The 1-3-1 overload set can also be used against this defense concentrating on the weakside roll maneuver.

Points of importance to remember when attacking this type of defense are:

1. Attack the defensive positioning by forcing the defense to adjust and change their pressure points.
2. Eliminate wasted guard-to-guard lateral exchanges.
3. Force the defense to readjust to unfamiliar positions by the player movement.
4. Create situations where the defensive players are unsure of their coverage responsibilities.

ATTACKING THE FRONTLINE ZONE

Another variation of a matchup zone is termed the frontline zone. Some teams employ a defense using the guards in a zone setup and the forwards and center playing man-for-man. These teams normally set up in a 2-3 formation which gives them great defensive strength around the basket and in the corner. Against this defense the 3-2, 1-3-1, and 1-3-1 overload sets are used primarily. Since the backline defense is playing man-for-man, each set is used independently and formed immediately each time down the floor.

There is no specific advantage in moving to the 1-3-1 from the 3-2 because the low defenders are playing man for man. It

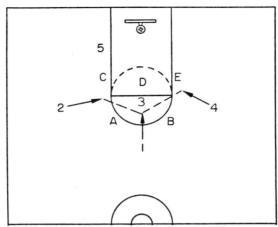

Diagram 9-10

is important that the point player takes the initiative by penetrating the defensive guards. From the 1-3-1 the point can penetrate to the foul line shooting behind 3 as a screen if C settles behind on defense. 1 can also pass off to the wings as A or B move tight to stop his penetration. The major points of penetration are the key and wing areas. (Diagram 9-10.)

When these opportunities are closed off, the normal continuity of the cut and roll options are run. The nature of this combination defense brings into effect a concept revolving around the "second man through." In all of the cut and roll maneuvers of the sets, there are two primary scoring threats — a player cutting to the basket and a player moving back through the defense as the cutter clears. In many cases the greatest potential is the second man filtering through the defense from behind. At times the possibility exists for a third man to be open as he flashes to an open spot and back to his normal position. However, this maneuver is an automatic response and takes place only momentarily, not to destroy the continuity of the pattern.

Points of importance to remember when attacking this type of defense are:

1. Split the even front defense for penetration possibilities with an odd front set.
2. Execute each maneuver completely to create openings and take advantage of all available players moving through the defense.
3. Utilize pattern continuity to keep the defense moving and in the process weaken their coverage responsibilities.

SUMMARY

In selecting the appropriate sets that will be most effective against situation zones, defensive analysis must first take place. This would be pinpointing the exact type of defensive setup being used. Next the proper sets selected are based on the even-odd concept of attacking. Using the multiple set then, three choices are available for each type of zone encountered. Depending on whether a high-low post, double low post, or single low post is needed will determine which choice to make.

Finally after designating the set to use, the type of offensive pressure applied will determine the proper options to emphasize. At times initial success will be thwarted. Confidence in the choice of sets employed along with proper execution will eventually produce openings to counteract any type of pressure employed by situation zones.

CHAPTER TEN

Multiple Set Adjustments to Combat Combination Defenses

The flexibility of zone defenses has made it necessary to develop offensive awareness and consequently incorporate offensive patterns to combat zone defensive variations. Many teams employ variations in their zone defenses as a change of pace, as a method of constant pressure on specific individuals, or to confuse the opponent. These variations include the box and 1, triangle and 2, and the diamond and 1. These are generally used in situations where a team possesses one or two outstanding players in the hope of upsetting the team's offensive continuity. The surprise element is extremely important in this type of defense. However, some teams have adopted this type of defense as their standard form. Further variations include alternating the assigned defender in the man situation each time down the floor. This gives the guarded player two distinct player types to be concerned with.

One popular theory is to place the player being guarded in the high post to force the box and 1 into a 2-1-2 alignment and attack with a 1-3-1 formation. However, there are disadvantages to doing so. In the first place the player may normally not operate from the high post position and consequently offensive continuity will be disrupted. Second, it will be difficult to give him the ball inside and therefore the best player will not be operating with the ball the majority of the time. Finally, many times the player will be completely ignored and the game becomes a four on four contest with the best player being eliminated from the competition. The defense then has the advantage because the best player is not a constant scoring threat. In counteracting this form of defensive pressure there are specific guidelines to follow in utilizing this player to advantage without disrupting offensive continuity.

1. The player does not change positions or basic movement, but only the side of the floor in relation to strongside or weakside concerning ball location. This eliminates confusion in terms of new responsibilities for positions. He can also be alternated from side to side in the same position depending upon where he seems to be most effective.

2. The player being guarded man-for-man initiates the offensive movement either with or without the ball. Since he is regarded as the chief threat, we want the other four players to become over concerned with him in hopes of pulling them out of position. Anxiety can be a tremendous factor in favor of the offense.

3. The player is isolated as much as possible in a 1 on 1 situation. A player demanding this type of coverage is certainly superior to the person guarding him. Hopefully he can be freed momentarily to operate for a good percentage shot. Two methods that have proven effective are to set up a screening situation for him with or without the ball, and place him in a low post position weakside to isolate him in a 1 on 1 rebounding situation off a teammate's shot.

4. The team is instructed to perform normal offensive movement to secure scoring opportunities. It is important not to become overconcerned about the variation in defense to the point of destroying pattern movement.

Multiple Set Adjustments to Combat Combination Defenses   *145*

5. The player being guarded man-for-man is designated as a primary offensive rebounder on all shots. This may appear strange but is actually sound offensive strategy for two main reasons. In the first place he is superior to the person guarding him and he may be able to pick up "garbage" baskets on errant rebounds. Second, should a fast break develop we don't want him picking up a foolish foul by stabbing a hand in as a last resort to prevent the shot, which might happen if he were a primary defender.

In the last five seasons we have had one player each year who has been a major reason for our success. Consequently we have faced a box and 1 defense on different occasions approximately 20% of the time. This has influenced us greatly in developing our basic sets to incorporate provisions to handle this type of defense with a minumum amount of adjustment to be made. Time is spent each week on this to avoid being caught off guard. I feel that the biggest trouble caused by this form of defense is the surprise element which can disrupt the offense and the confidence of the players to attack and defeat it. In considering the box and 1, it can be applied against a guard, a forward, or a center. However, the center and forwards in the multiple set operate under the same general offensive principles and the positions are interchangeable. Therefore, it only becomes necessary to consider the guard and forward positions in attacking this defense.

THE GUARD OPTION VS THE BOX AND 1 DEFENSE

The box and 1 has an even front and is attacked with an odd front set. The 3-2 set, 1-3-1 set, and 1-3-1 overload set are the available formations. For simplicity sake the player being contested man-for-man will be known as player x.

3-2 Baseline Screen Set

In this alignment x takes his basic position on the weakside wing opposite the initial penetration of the ball. x is allowed to bring the ball up at times on either side of the court. His movement allows the remaining four players ample time to adjust and know which side the penetration will originate from. As

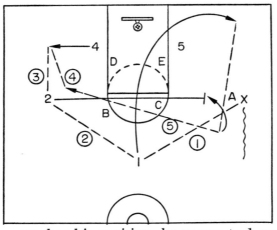

Diagram 10-1

x reaches his position, he passes to 1 on the point. 1 looks for penetration possibilities and passes to 2. 2 also looks for penetration and passes to 4 moving wide in the corner to initiate the cut option. 1 cuts through the middle of the defense looking for a return pass and moves to the opposite corner. After 1 clears, 2 immediately moves across to screen for x, who comes across and receives a pass from 4. This maneuver allows x to remain active by running his man into a screen. It also forces the defense to become aware of his movement and at times being drawn out of position. x quickly looks for an opening and shot. If nothing is available he passes to 2. 2 passes to 1 who has continued out into the corner. 1 looks for a shot or pass inside to 5 on the lane. (Diagram 10-1.) If I cannot find an opening he looks to pass back outside to take the movement to the other side. 2 screens across for x moving over to receive a pass from 1. x then passes to 2. 4 in the process moves into a tight lane position. 5 moves across the lane to the corner using

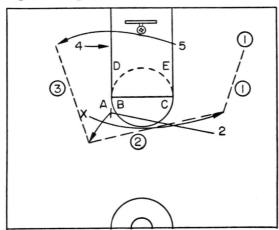

Diagram 10-2

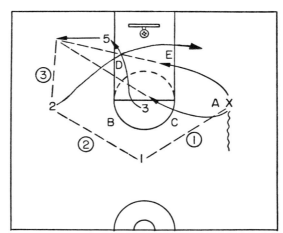

Diagram 10-3

4 as a screen. 2 passes to 4 for a shot or pass inside to 5. (Diagram 10-2.) This baseline screen maneuver continues until a good percentage shot is produced. Also, on each screen for x moving to receive a pass he is looking for a shooting opportunity.

1-3-1 Cut and Roll Set

Player x sets up in the normal weakside wing position. Once again x is allowed to bring the ball up the sideline. x proceeds to pass to the point after the ball is brought into offensive position. 1 passes to the strongside wing. 2 passes to 5 and cuts through the middle. As 2 clears, 3 rolls to a low post position same side. x makes his move beating the defender to an open spot in the lane and back out if he does not receive a pass. (Diagram 10-3.) A slight variation is placing x on the point position. As the initial pass into the corner is made, the weakside wing screens for x first before x makes his move into the lane area. (Diagram 10-4.)

Diagram 10-4

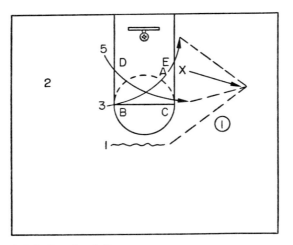

Diagram 10-5

1-3-1 Overload Set

Player x sets up in the weakside wing position tight on the lane. This allows x to maneuver for inside rebounding position on the shot developed in the passing option. Initiating the roll option by passing to x on the weakside allows him ample room to get open and receive a pass from 1. x quickly faces the basket on his reception to look for a shot preceeding the rolling action. (Diagram 10-5.) A variation would be 1 screening down for x on the return pass from the strongside wing. Upon reception x looks for a shot. x passes to 1 initiating the roll option. (Diagram 10-6.)

THE FORWARD OPTION VS THE BOX AND 1 DEFENSE

The three odd front sets are also used when a forward is being played man for man.

3-2 Baseline Screen Set

x lines up in a low post position opposite the side of the ball. x uses 5 as a screen and clears to the corner to receive a pass

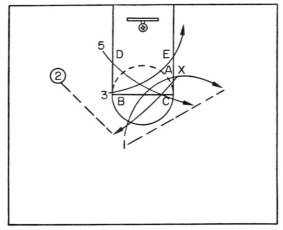

Diagram 10-6

Multiple Set Adjustments to Combat Combination Defenses

from the wing. As x clears, 5 slides across the lane to the normal low post position vacated by x. 3 passes into x and 1 cuts through to the opposite corner. By initiating the pattern with player x, this has a tendency to force the defense to overshift and move out of their basic defensive positioning to help cover x. x passes out to 3 adjusting. 3 passes to 2. 2 passes to 1 for a corner jumper or pass inside to 5. (Diagram 10-7.) The other alternative is to place x in the wing position as in the guard alignment. This all depends on whether x is a true forward or a swing player capable of playing both the guard and forward spots.

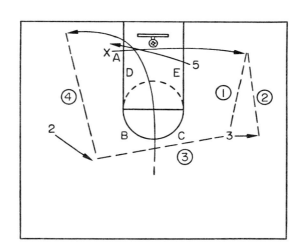

Diagram 10-7

1-3-1 Cut and Roll Set

If x is an inside forward primarily, he is placed in a high post position to force the defense into a 2-1-2 zone. From this the basic offense is run with concentration on ball movement and penetration from the point and wing positions. If x is a swing player, the alternative is to place him in the weakside wing position and run the pattern as described in the guard alignment.

1-3-1 Overload Set

In this set x can be stationed in one of three positions. If he has a definite size advantage, he assumes the low post position.

150 Multiple Set Adjustments to Combat Combination Defenses

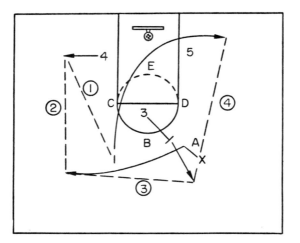

Diagram 10-8

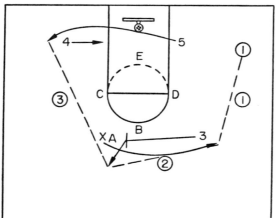

Diagram 10-9

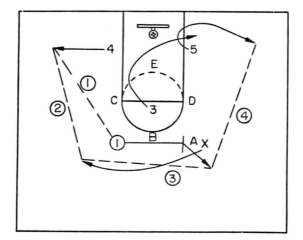

Diagram 10-10

Multiple Set Adjustments to Combat Combination Defenses   *151*

The strongside wing attempts to penetrate and feed off inside to x if he isn't fronted for a power move to the basket. The strongside wing can also feed the high post for a turn around jumper as the defense will sag to close off x. x can also move into the high post position. This can create openings for the strongside wing to penetrate, drive to the baseline and pass off inside, or pass to x if he isn't fronted. Finally, x can play the weakside wing and maneuver for good offensive rebounding position around the basket. He also initiates the roll option by clearing to the side as described earlier in the guard option.

THE GUARD OPTION VS THE DIAMOND AND 1 DEFENSE

The basic offensive zone principles apply to attacking the diamond and 1. This defense is characterized by an odd front and is therefore attacked with the 2-1-2, 2-2-1, or the 1-3-1 overload sets.

2-1-2 Permeter Set

x sets up in the guard position opposite the side of eventual penetration of the ball. x has the liberty and freedom to advance the ball up the sideline. This has the tendency to key the entire defense on his movement. Upon reaching his basic position, x passes across to the other guard. 1 passes into 4 moving out to the corner. 1 proceeds on his cut maneuver to the basket and out to the opposite corner. 3 backs out and screens for x to move across and receive a pass back from 4. x passes to 3. 3 passes to 1 in the corner for a shot or pass inside. (Diagram 10-8). When an open shot does not exist, 3 screens across for x to receive a pass back from 1. x passes to 3. 3 passes to 5 sliding along the baseline using 4 as a screen. 5 looks for the shot or pass inside to 4. (Diagram 10-9).

The roll option is started by x passing to 1. 1 passes into 4. 3 rolls to the basket and across the lane to the low post position. 5 loops as 3 clears and continues out to the corner. 1 screens for x to receive a pass back from 4. x passes to 1. 1 passes to 5 in the corner for a shot or pass inside to 3. (Diagram 10-10.)

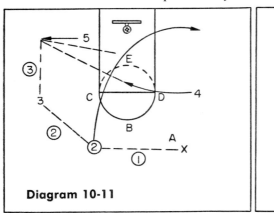
Diagram 10-11

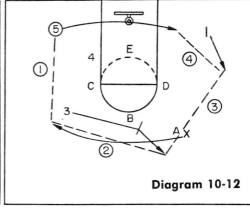
Diagram 10-12

2-2-1 Weakside Slide Set

x plays the weakside guard position opposite the side of eventual penetration. x passes to the other guard (1). 1 passes to 3. 3 passes to 5 and 1 cuts through the middle and out. As 1 clears, 4 comes back to the ball through the defense across the lane. (Diagram 10-11.) When nothing develops, 3 screens for x to receive a pass from 5. x passes to 3 who immediately delivers a pass to 1 in the corner for a shot or a pass inside to 5 sliding along the baseline. (Diagram 10-12.)

1-3-1 Overload Set

Player x assumes the weakside wing position. This alignment allows for good maneuverability around the basket for offensive rebounding purposes. The strongside wing position is very effective to produce good percentage shots. He can also draw defenders out to pass the ball inside to the high and low post

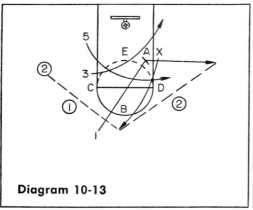
Diagram 10-13

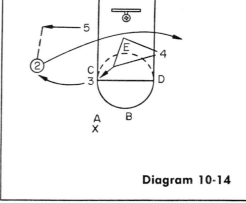
Diagram 10-14

Multiple Set Adjustments to Combat Combination Defenses   *153*

players. The roll option is implemented by having x break out wide for the ball on the weakside or by having 1 screen down for x to receive a pass from the strongside wing in the point position. (Diagram 10-13.)

When x is assigned to the point position initially, the primary offensive action consists of the strongside wing operating from the wing to the corner in conjunction with the high and low post. If 2 is covered, he can pitch the ball to 5 moving out for the release pass as the cutter rotation takes place. (Diagram 10-14.) However, in this situation x is completely out of the offensive picture. It is not advisable to use this unless the other players are capable of generating the major share of the offense.

THE FORWARD OPTION VS THE DIAMOND AND 1 DEFENSE

The 2-1-2, 2-2-1, and 1-3-1 overload sets are utilized when a forward is being played man-for-man in the diamond and 1 defense.

2-1-2 Perimeter Set

x is positioned in a low post position opposite the side of eventual penetration. The ball is controlled by the guard opposite x. This enables x to move along the baseline and use a screen to free himself to receive a pass. x moves across the lane using 4 to screen his man. After x clears, 4 slides across the lane to balance the offensive distribution. 1 passes to x and cuts through the defense continuing out to the opposite corner. Guard 2 adjusts to receive a pass back from x. 3 backs out to the top of the key and gets the pass from 2. 3 immediately passes to 1 in the corner for a shot or pass inside to 4 on the lane. (Diagram 10-15.)

If a shot does not develop the ball is passed back around the perimeter from 1-3-2. x meanwhile moves back to a tight lane position. 2 passes to 4 sliding along the lane to the corner using x as a screen. He has a fifteen-foot jump shot or pass inside to x if his defensive player is guarding from the rear. (Diagram 10-16.)

The roll option is initiated in the same fashion except the guard passing in holds his position. 3 rolls to a low post lane position.

154 *Multiple Set Adjustments to Combat Combination Defenses*

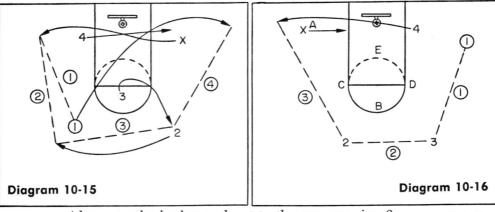

Diagram 10-15   Diagram 10-16

4 loops to the basket and out to the corner using 3 as a screen. x passes back to 1. 1 passes to 2 who passes immediately to 3 in the corner for the shot or drop in pass to 4 tight on the lane for a power move or hook shot. (Diagram 10-17.)

2-2-1 Weakside Slide Set

x plays the weakside wing position. Both guards and the strongside wing look for penetration points to split the defense. When openings do not exist, the cutter option is initiated by passing to the low post moving wide. 3 passes to 5 and 1 cuts through the defense and out to the opposite corner. After 1 clears, x moves to an open spot in the lane beating his defender and flashing into the low post looking for a pass. 5 passes back to 3. 3 passes to 2 adjusting his position. 2 passes immediately to 1 in the corner for a shot. (Diagram 10-18.)

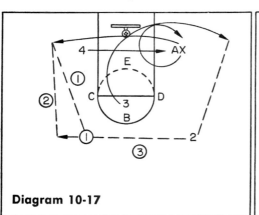   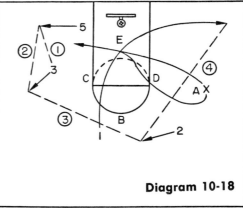

Diagram 10-17   Diagram 10-18

Multiple Set Adjustments to Combat Combination Defenses 155

1-3-1 Overload Set

x sets up in the weakside wing position and operates under the same principles outlined earlier in the guard option. However, his position will be confined primarily to the weakside wing or low post positions.

PLAYER MOVEMENT VS THE
ALTERNATING BOX AND 1 DEFENSE

An added variation in the box and 1 defense is to alternate the man-for-man pressure each time down the floor when a team possesses two players of equal ability. Once again this is attempted to confuse and disrupt the offensive tempo. In place of making numerous player adjustments each time down the floor, one specific set is utilized to combat this type of defense. The 1-3-1 overload set is the basic attack and has proven very successful for us against this defense. The offensive concentration is primarily generated through the passing option. The two players involved in this alternating form of defense play the weakside and strongside wing positions. The side of the floor assumed by these players has been pre-determined by previous game performance and spot shooting statistics in practice. It then becomes a minor adjustment to alternate the weak and strongside of the offense depending on the defensive pressure.

One particular team in our league employed this method of alternating the man-for-man pressure each time down the floor and we successfully forced them out of it after one quarter. The method was as follows: The original man for man pressure was on player 4, therefore the overload was setup strongside left with 4 playing the weakside wing on the right side. This allowed 2 to secure a good percentage shot from fifteen feet. It also allowed 4 to gain an offensive rebounding advantage close to the basket. (Diagram 10-19.)

After converting a shot, the next time down the floor defensive man-for-man pressure was applied on 2. If the defensive adjustment is diagnosed immediately as the ball is advanced up the floor, 3 and 5 simply slide across the lane to designate strongside right. 4 moves out to the strongside wing position and 2 moves into a tight lane position to become a weakside wing. If the de-

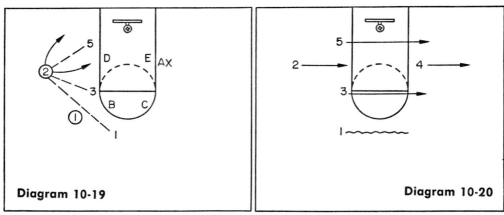

Diagram 10-19   **Diagram 10-20**

fensive change is not discovered until the offense is set up strongside left, the strongside is changed by running the normal roll option. 1 passes to 4 moving wide on the wing. 3 rolls to a low post position and 5 breaks into the lane and the high post position. 3 and 5 can then exchange high-low to resume their most effective positions. By changing the strongside it takes advantage of 4's ability to shoot from the right wing position. Diagrams 10-20 and 10-21 show the two methods of changing the strongside of the overload set.

The movement is basically simple but effective. It allows the opportunity to take advantage of specialized shooting abilities from the wing positions along with passing inside if the defense overshifts to shut off the strongside movement. Oftentimes in the process the defense momentarily loses sight of the low and high post which can produce inside scoring opportunities.

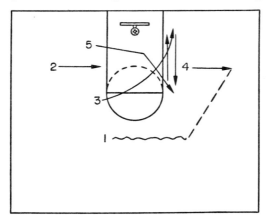

Diagram 10-21

Multiple Set Adjustments to Combat Combination Defenses   *157*

DOUBLE GUARD MOVEMENT VS THE
TRIANGLE AND 2 DEFENSE

The triangle and 2 defensive formation manifests itself in the concept of defensing the two best scorers man-for-man and zoning with the remaining three players in a triangle setup. This defense is capable of concentrating on two guards, two forwards, or one guard and one forward. It seldom includes a center due to his closeness to the basket and the offensive strength he possesses. If the apex of triangle is under the basket, the points of penetration are along the baseline as the remaining two players are at the foul line strengthening the defense in the wing areas. If the apex of the triangle is on the foul line, the major points of penetration are from the wing positions as the remaining two players in the triangle are assigned to the lane area around the basket protecting the base line.

When the defense is geared to stop two guards, the apex of the triangle is generally on the foul line. Offensive placement of the guards will result in the defense appearing as a 2-1-2 zone. However, the triangle has an odd front and is primarily attacked with an even front set. The 2-2-1 set with the strength in the wings is the one most often used. x1 and x2 play normal guard positions. An important note to interject at this time is attacking the triangle and 2 defense. The nature of the defense closes off the lane area initially in good balance. Therefore, the most productive opportunities secured are the second and third players moving after the basic cut and roll movement is started. This is true because the defense has a tendency to forget players behind them to anticipate coverage responsibilities. Players filtering back through the defense towards the ball become effective offensive tools.

2-2-1 Weakside Slide Set

In the 2-2-1 set the guards are instructed to screen as often as possible for one another. This will force the defense to work harder along with providing an uncomfortable contact situation. I find that teams employing this defense have the defenders constantly talking and harassing their opponents. The only opportunity the offensive players have to gain an advantage is by running the defenders into screens as often as possible. This

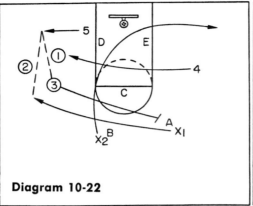
Diagram 10-22

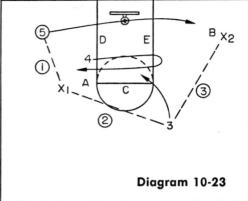
Diagram 10-23

definitely becomes a factor in eliminating hostilities being built up by the players by not being able to retaliate. Anytime a guard passes into the wing position he automatically screens away from the ball to create more player movement. A wing can penetrate when receiving a pass, pass back to the other guard, or pass to the low post initiating the cutter option. 3 passes to 5 in the corner. x2 being the second man from the ball cuts through to the opposite corner. As x2 clears, 4 moves back through the defense across the lane looking for a pass. 3 screens for x1 to come across for a return pass from 5 if nothing develops. Diagram 10-22. 5 passes to x1. x1 passes to 3. 3 looks to penetrate and then passes to x2 in the corner or to 4 flashing in the lane and out again. 5 is also available by sliding along the base line under the basket. (Diagram 10-23.)

3 slides down to screen for x1 moving back out to his original position and the offense is ready to operate once again.

2-1-2 Perimeter Set

The 2-1-2 set is an alternate formation to use. This forces the defense into a 2-1-2 defense. Concentration is on the roll option to free a forward in the corner for a shot or baseline penetration. x1 passes to 4 and screens away for x2. 3 rolls to the basket and opposite low post position. 5 loops to the basket and out to the corner. 4 passes back to x2 who is free from the screen by x1. x1 fakes toward the basket and steps back for a pass from x2. x1 passes to 5 in the corner for a shot or look inside to 3 on the lane if the defense is playing behind him. (Diagram 10-24.) If nothing develops, the adjustment is simply 3 moving back into the high post to start the offensive action again.

Multiple Set Adjustments to Combat Combination Defenses

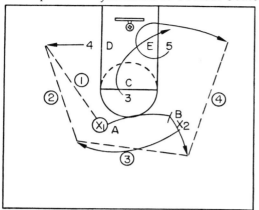

Diagram 10-24

GUARD-FORWARD MOVEMENT VS THE TRIANGLE AND 2 DEFENSE

In this setup man-for-man pressure is applied on a guard and a forward. The most effective set is the 1-3-1 overload set with the 2-2-1 set being an alternate formation.

1-3-1 Overload Set

The guard (x1) assumes the point position. The forward (x2) assumes the weakside wing position for primarily rebounding purposes. Many shot opportunities are presented from the strongside position. If the defense overshifts to cover 2, 3, and 5, the ball is quickly reversed for x1 and x2 to work two-man situations. x1 and x2 can work a pick-and-roll maneuver with x2 moving up to set up a screen for x1. x1 and x2 can work a two-man weave for jump shots, or x1 can dribble to the weakside position initiating the roll option. This is effective since the defense has already committed themselves to overshifting to cover the strongside setup.

2-2-1 Weakside Slide Set

x1 sets up in the weakside guard position and advances the ball up the floor. x2 sets up in the weakside forward position. x1 and x2 can work two man situations mentioned above when possible. To initiate the cutter option, x1 passes to the other guard. The pass moves to 4, then to 5 in the corner. 2 initiates his cut to the basket and out to the opposite corner. x2 makes his move into the lane from his weakside wing position after 2 clears looking for an opening. When neither opportunity is available,

4 screens across for x1 to move over and receive a pass back from 5. x1 passes to 4 stepping back. 4 passes to 2 in the corner for a shot or pass inside to 5 sliding along the baseline under the basket. (Diagram 10-25.)

DOUBLE FORWARD MOVEMENT VS THE TRIANGLE AND 2 DEFENSE

In this situation man-for-man pressure is applied to both forwards. If the forwards occupy a low post position, the apex of the triangle defense will be under the basket and thus forming almost a 2-3 alignment. The set used is the 2-1-2 formation.

2-1-2 Perimeter Set

This set enables the forwards being played man-for-man to remain close to the basket in good rebounding position. Penetration at a forty-five degree angle by the guards is possible and passing inside to the high post can be effective if the defense is behind.

Offensive action begins with a guard passing to x1 or x2 moving wide to the corner. They free each other by sliding along the baseline using one another for a screen. The guard passing in has the option of cutting or staying. If the guard cuts, the opposite guard adjusts for a return pass. 3 steps towards the ball first for a quick pass and then moves out to the top of the key to receive a pass from 2. x2 passes to 2. 2 passes to 3. 3 passes to 1 in the corner for a shot or pass inside to x1 if defense is behind. (Diagram 10-26.) If a shot is not available, 1 passes back to 3. 3 passes to 2. 2 passes to x1 moving back

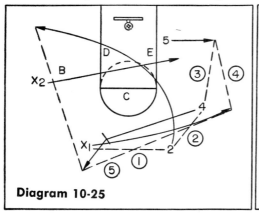

Diagram 10-25

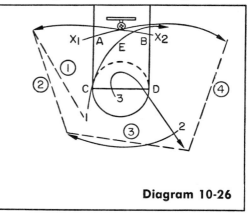

Diagram 10-26

Multiple Set Adjustments to Combat Combination Defenses 161

across the lane using x2 for a screen. If 1 holds his position after passing to x2 in the corner, 3 rolls to a low post position looking for a pass. x2 passes back to 1. 1 passes to 2. 2 passes to x1 who has looped into the lane and back to the corner using 3 for a screen. x1 immediately looks for a shot or pass inside to 3 who in most cases will have the defense playing behind him. (Diagram 10-27.) If nothing develops, the ball is reversed around the horn to catch 3 sliding along the baseline to the corner off x2 for the shot.

Diagram 10-27

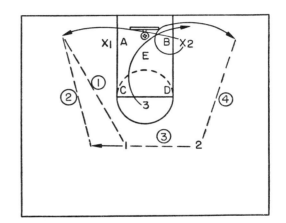

SUMMARY

The previous patterns analyzed in attacking zone defensive variations have proven successful for us. They include refinements only and not drastic changes in the multiple set zone offense. Specific sets will be emphasized at times with player positioning important in making them strong offensive tools. The one single important element for success is confidence that the patterns will produce openings for the players to score. Confidence is based on a certain degree of success previously achieved in this area and the knowledge that there are elements specifically designed to attack each form of zone defensive variation encountered. Once the multiple set zone offense has been implemented, adjustments to compensate for defensive changes in strategy will be easily seen by the players.

The patterns covered in attacking the zone variations encompass all possible alternatives. However, they will be limited based on the evaluation of the personnel involved along with the tendencies of the defense employed. Subjective evaluation by the coach will narrow down the material necessary to be employed to be successful. By the time a team encounters any of the defensive tactics covered, the strengths of the key offensive player(s) will be known to determine which set and option to use.

CHAPTER ELEVEN

Developing Shooting and Passing Techniques Against Zone Defenses

In the area of shooting techniques there are many important points to be analyzed in terms of attacking zone defenses. It is very difficult to gain an offensive advantage in a 1 on 1 situation, hard to find a driving lane clear, difficult to screen for a teammate, and extremely hard at times to penetrate the lane area. Therefore, the importance of getting to the outside shooting position quickly, efficiently, and effectively to provide good scoring opportunities is necessary to be successful against zone defenses.

EMPLOYING A SHOOTING INDEX

In our system of play we find it necessary to emphasize percentage shooting since we encounter a zone defense 85-90 percent of the time. To aid us in this we have instituted a shooting index for our players. After analyzing all of our games in the past five seasons, 40% shooting from the field and 70% shooting from the foul line would have resulted in winning 95% of all games on a pure shooting basis. The first step was to keep a shooting record each day to determine each player's

163

164 Developing Shooting and Passing Techniques Against Zone Defenses

best and poorest shooting areas in terms of the percentage of shots made. Charts were kept in both drills and scrimmage sessions.

Second, we kept extensive shooting statistics in all pre-season scrimmages on each player comparing them with their practice percentage areas. Third, we took game shooting statistics and attempted to isolate percentages that would have resulted in the greatest number of wins and at the same time setting a realistic goal for each individual player to achieve.

The results of this indicated that the percentages of 70 for foul shooting and 40 for field goal shooting were realistic and reachable for each player. These percentages of course are geared to the caliber of competition being played and based on the team's past performances and capabilities. The percentages would vary accordingly for another team in another situation on a different level of competition. Based on these percentages the method of computing each players *shooting index* would be: Total Points Scored − (70% foul shooting attempts + 40% field goal attempts) = Shooting Index. Therefore, a player in a game shooting 7-10 (70%) from the foul line and 4-10 (40%) from the field would receive a shooting index of 0. Examples would be:

Player	Total Points	Foul Shooting	Field Goals	Shooting Index
A	18	6-10	6-10	+ 3.0
B	14	8-10	3-10	− 1.0
C	5	3-4	1-1	+ 1.4
D	7	3-6	2-6	− 2.0

Player A: In taking 10 foul shots, he should have scored 7 points (70%). By making 6 or 60% of his attempts he has a -1.0 in foul shooting (7-6). In taking 10 shots from the field he needed to make at least 4 field goals (8 points) to achieve the 40% factor. He made 6 field goals (60%). Therefore he scored 4 more points than was necessary to achieve a 0 in the shooting index. His field goal shooting index was + 4.0. Total shooting index was + 3.0 (-1 for foul shooting, + 4 for field goals).

Developing Shooting and Passing Techniques Against Zone Defenses 165

Player B: 8 for 10 from the foul line (80%) gives a +1 because he made one more than 70% (7-10). 3 for 10 from the field is less than 40%. He scored 6 points but should have scored 8. Consequently his field goal index was -2.0. Total shooting index was -1.0 (+1 for foul shooting and -2 for field goal shooting).

Player C: 3 for 4 from the line equals 75%. 70% of 4 shots taken is 2.8 Therefore his foul shooting index was +.2 (3-2.8). 1 for 1 from the field is 100%. 40% of 1 field goal or 2 points is .8. 2 − .8 = +1.2 Total shooting index is +1.4 (+.2 for foul shooting and +1.2 for field goal shooting).

Player D: 3 for 6 from the foul line is 50%. 70% of 6 attempts is 4.2. Therefore his foul shooting index is -1.2 (3-4.2). 2 for 6 from the field is 33%. 40% of 6 is 2.4 field goals or 4.8 points. He should have scored 9 points total for the game. He scored 7 and therefore his shooting index was −2.0 (−1.2 from foul shooting and −.8 from field goal shooting).

All players are striving for a plus factor in their shooting index. This indicates a player is scoring more points than is computed necessary according to the number of shots he attempted in a game. The eventual hope is for the team as a whole to shoot an index of at least 0 but preferably of course on the plus side. We have used the shooting index to improve our accuracy as well as a method of explaining the importance of taking good percentage shots. Varsity basketball players should achieve a 0 index without much difficulty. However, when a player is receiving a negative index he is made to realize he is committing one of four major faults in shooting.

1. Taking a poor percentage shot for his ability.
2. Forcing a shot.
3. Rushing a shot.
4. Taking a shot outside of his shooting range.

If a condition exists where a player continually has a negative shooting index, an individual conference is in order to advise and individually improve his overall shooting game. Since in-

166 Developing Shooting and Passing Techniques Against Zone Defenses

corporating this method of using a shooting index the following results have been realized:

1. The overall team shooting percentage has improved.
2. Players become more aware of team play by taking better percentage shots as opposed to placing total emphasis on the amount of points scored. (We successfully defended our league championship for three years running with only one returning starter in the latter two seasons.)
3. Each player has a chance to receive offensive recognition with this system.

The highest shooting index a player has ever achieved for us in one game was 11.6. His shooting totals included 8-8 from the foul line and 9-11 from the field.

SIX POINTERS TO IMPROVE OUTSIDE SHOOTING AGAINST ZONE DEFENSES

1. **Body Position**

   A. Assume a stable position with the knees slightly bent to keep the center of gravity well in control of the body to move to the shooting position quickly and efficiently.
   B. Step with the outside foot to meet the pass designating the rear foot as the pivot foot to be in position to face the basket for the shot or to reverse pivot and protect the ball from defensive pressure.
   C. Upon reception of the pass, close up the stance for balance. The feet are parallel, shoulders squared away to the basket, and the weight evenly distributed and ready to initiate the shot.

2. **Ball Position**

   A. Upon receiving the pass and squaring the body to the basket, the ball is placed in a position about waist level to develop an offensive threat.
   B. The four options available are a shot, pass, fake and drive, or a pivot to protect the ball from pressure.
   C. The hands are always in the same position on the ball to protect the defense from anticipating the offensive maneuver.

Developing Shooting and Passing Techniques Against Zone Defenses 167

3. **Quick Release**

   A. Moving the ball from the offensive threat position to the shooting position quickly and efficiently, enabling the shooter to concentrate on the completion of the shot and follow through.

4. **Concentration**

   A. Devoting 100% attention on the target (rim) without showing concern for the tactics of distraction employed by the defense.

Tactics such as rushing the offense to shoot, timed shouting, and waving the hands high to present an obstacle to shoot over are common to zone defenses. It is worthwhile to present these conditions in practice to prepare the players for this type of diversion. One method is to have the players shoot over a volleyball net as an obstacle. Another method is to pair off players at each basket. One player passes the ball and then charges the shooter, attempting to cause a fumble or rush the shot. A third method would be to station players in groups of three at each basket. One player passes to a second player who is the shooter. As he is attempting the shot, the third player waves his hands and attempts to distract the shooter by timing a shout at the moment of release. Players are rotated to assume each position and responsibilities.

5. **Shooting Range**

A shot should not have to be taken outside the 18 foot perimeter in high school basketball with the exception of a last-second desperation shot. With proper ball movement and patience against a zone defense, a shot inside that distance will be the end result. We feel any shot taken from beyond this range by the average high school basketball player is considered a poor percentage shot. To analyze the shooting range of each player, we chart and record daily the number of shots taken from specific spots designated on the floor. With this method we have found a great deal of difference between the shooting range capabilities of each individual team member. Players are required to record the number of shots made and also to achieve a certain percentage that we attach to each spot.

168 Developing Shooting and Passing Techniques Against Zone Defenses

The number of shots taken daily will vary to improve the concentration of the players as well as maintaining interest. The percentages achieved of course are much higher than would be expected from that spot in a game, but it gives the players an indication of where they have the best chance of scoring along with supplying the coaching staff with data to discuss with the players their individual shooting weaknesses.

6. Percentage Shooting:

This area overlaps the area of shooting range and the same charts can indicate the player's shooting strengths and weaknesses. If a player takes a shot from one of his weaker areas, it is considered a poor percentage shot for his capabilities.

Each individual set formation of the multiple set zone offense has a passing option to take advantage of spot shooting. If a team is showing poor recovery of the ball on defense, we will elect to concentrate on our passing option without cutting any players through the defense. By knowing the strong shooting areas of the players and their individual preference for a shot, it is very easy to make the minor adjustment of placing the players in their strongest shooting positions. An example of this is very evident in using the 1-3-1 overload set. One season we had two boys of equal shooting ability on an overall percentage basis. Normally the overload is to the left with the majority of shots originating from the left wing position. The two players would alternate in this position depending upon who had the hotter shooting hand. However, one of the players continually shot a better percentage from the left wing. After analyzing the shooting charts it was apparent that the other player was a much better shooter from the right wing position. After discovering this it was a simple matter to reverse the overload from side to side depending upon the player selected as the key shooter. It also simplified the offensive pattern against a situation defense such as the box and one. Depending on which player was being played man-for-man, he would be shifted to the weakside wing position opposite the overload. This offensive adjustment will be covered in detail in Chapter 11 on zone defensive variations.

Developing Shooting and Passing Techniques Against Zone Defenses 169

SHOOTING DRILLS

In the area of fundamentals there are certain drills related to specifically increasing scoring opportunities against zone defenses. These relate to passing and shooting drills while attempting to eliminate unnecessary dribbling and wasted motion. In terms of shooting we emphasize controlled shooting drills, concentrating on the various spots of the floor where the majority of good percentage shots will be obtained in each option of each set.

1. Quick Release Drill

For each offensive set there is a passing option and a series of two-man shooting drills that can be isolated to improve each player's individual shooting ability. In these two-player exchange situations three passes are used. The pass starts from the passer to the intended shooter. The shooter returns the pass and then receives a second pass at which time he goes up for the shot. By incorporating three passes both boys are kept active during the drill along with improving the shooter's ability to receive the ball and quickly get it to the shooting position without fumbling the ball or wasting a dribble. Each player receives three shots and then positions are exchanged. Players are rotated to different areas to continue the drill. In all there are sixty-four variations for the two man drills. Generally, concentration should be on one offensive set and the two-man situations before moving on to the other sets. Referral to earlier diagrams numbering the positions in the various sets will eliminate unnecessary diagrams now.

A. Two player combinations in the 1-3-1 set include:

1) Point-Left Wing Left Wing-Point
2) Point-Right Wing Right Wing-Point
3) Point-High Post High Post-Point
4) Left Wing-Low Post Low Post-Left Wing
5) Right Wing-Low Post Low Post-Right Wing
6) Left Wing-High Post High Post-Left Wing
7) Right Wing-High Post High Post-Right Wing
8) High Post-Low Post Left Low Post Left-High Post
9) High Post-Low Post Right Low Post Right-High Post

170 Developing Shooting and Passing Techniques Against Zone Defenses

B. Two player combinations in the 2-1-2 set include:

1)	Left Guard-Right Guard	Right Guard-Left Guard
2)	Left Guard-High Post	High Post-Left Guard
3)	Right Guard-High Post	High Post-Right Guard
4)	Left Guard-Low Post	Low Post-Left Guard
5)	Right Guard-Low Post	Low Post-Right Guard
6)	High Post-Left Low Post	Left Low Post-High Post
7)	High Post-Right Low Post	Right Low Post-High Post

C. Two player combinations in the 3-2 set include:

1)	Point-Left Wing	Left Wing-Point
2)	Point-Right Wing	Right Wing-Point
3)	Left Wing-Low Post	Low Post-Left Wing
4)	Right Wing-Low Post	Low Post-Right Wing

D. Two player combinations in the 2-2-1 set include:

1)	Left Guard-Right Guard	Right Guard-Left Guard
2)	Left Guard-Wing	Wing-Left Guard
3)	Right Guard-Wing	Wing-Right Guard
4)	Left Wing-Low Post	Low Post-Left Wing
5)	Right Wing-Low Post	Low Post-Right Wing

E. Two player combinations in the 1-3-1 overload set include:

1)	Point-Strongside Wing Left	Strongside Wing Left-Point
2)	Point-Strongside Wing Right	Strongside Wing Right-Point
3)	Point-Weakside Wing Left	Weakside Wing Left-Point
4)	Point-Weakside Wing Right	Weakside Wing Right-Point
5)	Point-High Post Left	High Post Left-Point
6)	Point-High Post Right	High Post Right-Point
7)	Strongside Wing-Low Post	Low Post-Strongside Wing

2. Pass and Press Drill

This drill requires four players stationed at a basket with one player at the top of the circle, one player under the basket, and the other two players in wide corner positions 15'-18' from the basket. Diagram 11-1 shows the position of the players in organizing the pass and press drill.

Player 1 starts off with the ball and passes to player 2, 3 or 4. As soon as the pass is released he charges the shooter with his hands high and shouting for distraction. The shooter

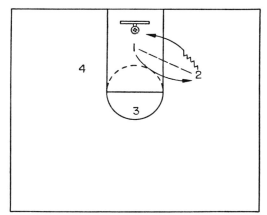

Diagram 11-1

upon receiving the ball immediately takes the jump shot under control. After the shot he follows to the basket. If the shot went in he passes to one of the two remaining players and follows, performing the same tactics of distracting the shooter and replacing him in that position. If the jump shot did not go in, the shooter follows and makes the rebound layup first before continuing the drill. The drill can continue for any length of time with the rotation of the players to different shooting areas. It is terminated by a time limit or by making a specific number of shots.

3. Around the Horn

This drill emphasizes the basic positions in the offensive sets that make up the multiple set offense. The teams are set up with one at each end of the court. The ball always starts from the point position in the odd front sets (1-3-1, 1-3-1 overload, and 3-2) and a guard position in the even front sets (2-1-2, and 2-2-1). This is done because the offensive pattern is initiated from these points. On the coach's whistle the ball is passed around the horn in any direction as quickly as possible. On a second whistle the next player receiving the pass immediately squares himself to the basket in good shooting position and takes the shot. Restrictions on the drill include no dribbling and passing only to the next person on the left, right, front, or rear of the passer. Various forms of competition can be organized. The last team to make the shot runs a lap. It can also be run at the conclusion of practice with the first team making five shots showering up without sprints. Generally only one offensive set should be emphasized per practice session. This eliminates boredom,

172 *Developing Shooting and Passing Techniques Against Zone Defenses*

saves time, and concentrates on one offensive formation. Refer to previous diagrams for the basic positioning of players in the various sets to conduct the drill.

4. Spot Shooting Drill

Shooting spots are marked on the floor according to the positions determined by the offensive sets. There is an overlapping of spots when the five sets are marked. In total there are sixteen shooting spots outlined. A daily record of shots made is kept for all players. Every player is required to shoot from every spot and many times a player may be found to be an outstanding shooter from one specific spot on the floor. This information can be invaluable against a zone defense as well as determining the logical choice for a last second shot. Different methods can be employed to record the shots to give variation and add fun to the practice session. One method is to set a percentage requirement from each spot. A second method would be to take a certain number of shots from each spot and record an overall percentage of shots made. A third method would be to shoot one shot from each spot to determine which player can make the most baskets out of the required number taken. A fourth method would be to find out which player takes the least number of shots to make one basket at each of the sixteen spots. Diagram 11-2 illustrates the sixteen shooting spots which appear in all the sets. The numbers in the circles refer to the repetition of spots in the various sets. The key is self-explanatory in analyzing the various spots.

Key for shooting spots:
1-3-1 set (1)
2-1-2 set (2)
3-2 set (3)
2-2-1 set (4)
overload (5)

5. Contact Drill

Contact is inherent in the game of basketball whether it is intentional or accidental. Therefore it is important that the players become accustomed to some type of contact on the jump shot which will happen during the fast-paced action of a game. A follow-the-leader type jump shooting line is formed from

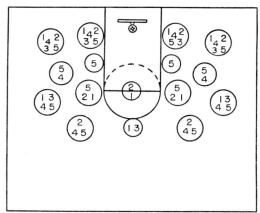

Diagram 11-2

various areas of the court. The first player dribbles up to the coach and takes a jump shot. During the shot the coach makes some form of contact with the shooter attempting to disturb his concentration. The methods used are those most likely to occur in a game.

1. Slap on the wrist
2. Hack on the arm
3. Knudge the hip
4. Jab at the stomach

It is important that the coach causes the contact. Sometimes players if allowed to cause the contact may create hard feelings because of the degree used. Diagram 11-3 shows the basic alignment for the drill.

6. **5-10-15 Drill**

A final jump-shooting drill specifically used to prepare against zone defenses is the 5-10-15 drill. Semi-circles around the basket are formed. Generally two baskets are used dividing the squad in half. Both groups start at a five foot arc. Every player shoots a

Diagram 11-3

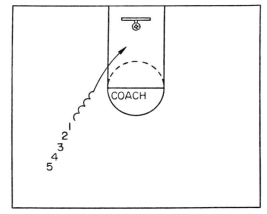

174 Developing Shooting and Passing Techniques Against Zone Defenses

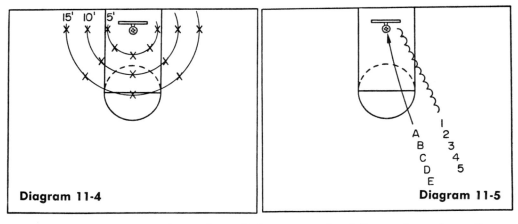

predetermined number of shots at each of five points along the arc. After everyone has rotated the players move back to the second semi-circle at 10'. The same procedure is followed and then to 15'. A certain number of shots or a specific time limit dictates when the players change positions. The rotation should be from both left to right, and right to left at different times for variation. Diagram 11-4 illustrates the three arcs around the basket to perform the drill.

Layups are extremely important in basketball and many are missed which might have been converted into three-point plays. Particularly against a zone when the defense is keying the ball, layups present themselves for only a split second and then under a situation where contact usually occurs. We have a series of layup drills designed to create situations similar to those occurring during a game.

7. Aggressive Layup Drill

This drill is designed to give the offensive player a half-step advantage on the defense. The object of the drill is to teach the offensive player to drive in a straightline path to the basket ignoring the efforts of the defensive player. In most cases some sort of contact will occur as the defensive player recovers and attempts to prevent the layup. Two lines are formed at the top of the foul circle. The offensive player has a half-step advantage and proceeds to fake the defensive player out of position and drives for the basket. After the play both players exchange lines. The drill is run from the left side, right side,

Developing Shooting and Passing Techniques Against Zone Defenses 175

left baseline, and right baseline. Diagram 11-5 shows player positioning for the aggressive layup drill.

8. Down the Middle Layup Drill

All players should be taught the art of taking the ball up with two hands off the dribble and penetrating the defense for a layup and possible three-point play. A line of players is stationed at midcourt. Two players are stationed opposite each other across the foul lane about eight feet from the basket. Their outside foot must remain on the foul lane with their inside arm outstretched across the lane. The first player at midcourt starts dribbling towards the basket. As he approaches the defenders, he plants his right foot and picks up the ball off the dribble stepping on to his left foot and going up for the layup. If the player misses the layup or fails to stay inbounds to rebound his own missed shot, he is assigned a certain number of layups at a side basket before joining the drill again. The players perform this drill dribbling and shooting the layup with both the left and right hand. Diagram 11-6 outlines the position of players for the down the middle layup drill.

9. Loose Ball Layup Drill

An important area of basketball deals with the ability of a player to react to a loose ball on the floor around the offensive basket, locate the basket, and jump towards the basket to complete a layup. In the loose ball layup drill two boys are paired off at each basket with two balls placed on the floor within five feet of the basket. Player 1 picks up one of the balls and jumps from that spot to the basket for a layup. As soon as he releases the shot and returns to the floor, he locates the second ball and continues to jump towards the basket for a layup. Meanwhile Player 2 is rebounding the shot and placing the extra ball at some other point on the floor. Player 1 continues reacting, jumping and shooting a layup ten times. Player 2 then becomes the shooter and 1 the rebounder. Diagram 11-7 shows the position of the players around the basket to perform the drill.

10. Double-Team Layup Drill

This drill teaches the players to secure an offensive rebound and go right back up for the shot through a defensive double-

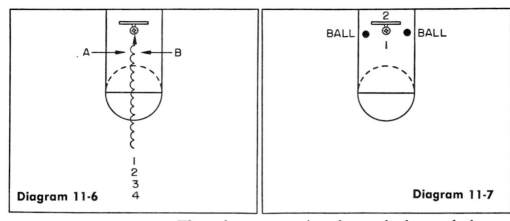

team attempt. Three boys are assigned to a basket and they rotate after each attempt. Player 2 stands with the ball facing the backboard at a distance of five feet from the basket. Player 2 stands in front of Player 1 also facing the basket. Player 3 stands under the backboard facing Player 2. Player 1 tosses the ball off the backboard and Player 2 jumps to rebound the ball. As he lands on the floor Players 1 and 3 attempt to double-team and knock the ball out of Player 2's hands. Player 2 immediately attempts to break through the double-team and score the layup. Players rotate from 1 to 2 to 3 and use both sides of the basket for the drill. Diagram 11-8 shows the initial setup of players for this drill.

There are three layup drills we use to improve the players' timing around the basket. Since traffic is generally very heavy in the lane area, oftentimes an opening only exists for a split second. Therefore it is advantageous for every player to develop the ability to recognize this situation and convert it into a score.

11. Jumping Layup Drill

The first of these timing drills consists of making ten consecutive jumping layups. As soon as the player rebounds the shot he releases for the next attempt. Two boys are assigned to a basket and alternate in sets of ten. The series of ten attempts are:

    a) ten layups from the right side with the right hand
    b) ten layups from the left side with the left hand
    c) ten layups from the right side with the left hand
    d) ten layups from the left side with the right hand

Developing Shooting and Passing Techniques Against Zone Defenses 177

After the players can perform these fairly well, another variation consists of switching sides of the basket on each attempt.

12. **Two Man Tapping Drill**

The second timing drill consists of two players paired off at a basket with one on either side. They toss the ball back and forth over the basket off the backboard alternating tapping the ball in and rebounding the ball and going back up for the layup. After a set number of attempts or a time limit, players exchange sides and continue the drill. Diagram 11-9 shows the position of the players in this drill.

13. **Airborne Layup Drill**

This drill teaches the players to receive a pass in the air in the vicinity of the basket and convert it into a score. One line is formed in the corner and another line is formed at the top of the foul circle. The first player in the corner line breaks along the baseline. As he approaches the basket, the first player in the passing line throws a lob pass towards the basket. The cutter leaps and catches the ball in the air. He gains control of his body, locates the basket, and lays the ball in before returning to the floor. If he cannot achieve this, he must recognize his poor position to the basket and return to the floor without shooting. As soon as he gathers himself he goes right back up for the layup. Variations of the drill include:

    a) cutting line left corner — passing line right wing
    b) cutting line right corner — passing line left wing

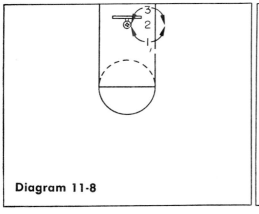

Diagram 11-8

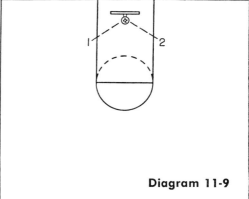

Diagram 11-9

178 Developing Shooting and Passing Techniques Against Zone Defenses

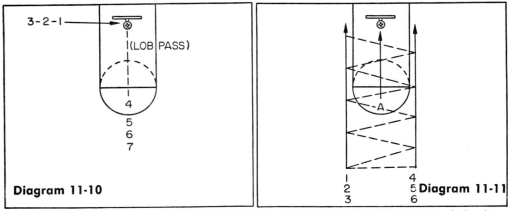

c) cutting line right corner — passing line top of foul circle
d) cutting line left corner — passing line top of foul circle

Diagram 11-10 shows the player lineup for the drill.

Passing is the most important single ingredient in gaining success against a zone defense. Failure to execute the correct pass for the situation will result in many missed scoring attempts. In practice it is difficult to motivate varsity players to concentrate on improving their passing technique and to recognize the proper pass to use in a situation unless a certain amount of variation and fun are employed.

14. Two on One Passing Drill

Two lines are formed at midcourt about twelve feet apart facing one another. A defensive player is stationed at the top of the foul circle. The first player from both lines starts sliding towards the basket passing the ball back and forth, employing both the chest and bounce passes. When they reach the top of the circle the defensive man attempts to intercept the pass. The offensive players continue passing to the basket for the layup. No dribbling is allowed. If the ball is deflected or intercepted by the defensive player, the player who passed the ball moves to a side wall and throws ten passes of the same type that was intercepted. Each defensive player receives three or four attempts and then becomes an offensive player. Diagram 11-11 shows the formation of players for this drill.

Developing Shooting and Passing Techniques Against Zone Defenses 179

15. **Perimeter Passing Drill**

Five lines two or three deep are set up in a spread formation. (Diagram 11-12.)

Two balls are used in this drill starting with Players 1 and 5. On a command or whistle 1 passes to 2 to 4 and 5 passes to 3 to 1. When the balls reach the corner and the point position, they reverse back to the other side. As soon as the ball is passed by Players 2-3-4 and 5, they step out and move to the end of their line. Player 1 passes twice before he moves to the end of his line. The object is to move the ball as quickly and accurately as possible. If one ball is moving slower than the other, Player 1 is liable to be hit with two passes at the same time. After a period of time each group is moved to the different positions around the perimeter and the drill continues. Both bounce and chest passes are used.

16. **Zig Zag Passing Drill**

This drill incorporates concentration and execution to keep the passes moving smoothly. The object is for each player to pass and receive the balls and not be concerned with anything or anyone else. Two equal lines of players are formed facing each other about ten feet apart. Diagram 11-13 shows the alignment.

Players 1 and 2 each have a ball. The even line passes a bounce pass to the first player to his left in the odd line. The odd line passes a two-hand chest pass to the first person to his right in the even line. The two balls continue down the line with even

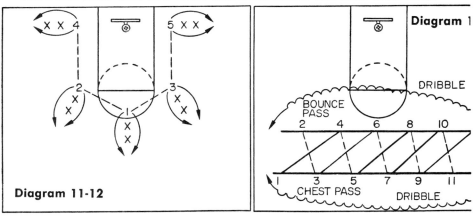

180 Developing Shooting and Passing Techniques Against Zone Defenses

side throwing bounce passes and the odd line throwing chest passes. When the balls reach the last two players, they dribble to the front of the line as fast as they can to start passing again. After the drill is running smoothly, two more balls are added to the drill. As the skill increases six and eight balls may be used. This drill adds some fun to the daily practice devoted to passing improvement.

Two other passing drills used specifically in preparing against a zone defense are geared to the idea of impressing the players to use a variety of passes and deception to complete a pass when a defensive man splits two or more offensive players, making it difficult for a clear pass.

17. Man in the Middle Passing Drill

This drill involves six players in a group. Five players form a circle and the sixth player positions himself in the middle of the circle on defense. The object of the defensive man is to intercept or deflect a pass from one of the players in the circle. The player whose pass was deflected replaces the man in the middle on defense. The passing rules for the five players include:

a) the ball cannot be passed to the next player on the right or left, therefore only two passing possibilities for each player exist.
b) all passes must be thrown below the head of the defender
c) if a pass is too hard or too wild for the receiver to handle, he replaces the man in the middle.

Diagram 11-14 shows the lineup of players in this drill.

18. Split the Offense Drill

This drill is run in groups of three. Two players stand about twelve feet apart passing the ball back and forth. The third player plays in between the other two attempting to deflect or intercept the ball. When the ball is deflected, the player making the error becomes the defensive man. Sometimes a defensive player is unable to deflect the pass, in which case a time limit would be set on the drill.

In all of the above drills the emphasis is on execution. A long time should not be spent on each individual drill to eliminate boredom and a lack of concentration by the players. Variation in drills is the key to learning basketball fundamentals.

Developing Shooting and Passing Techniques Against Zone Defenses 181

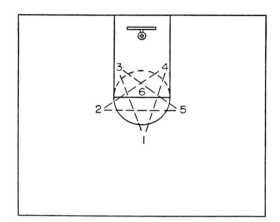

Diagram 11-14

It should be noted that these drills outlined are only used in a maximum of ten practice sessions, as are all other individual fundamental drills. Different drills accomplish the same objectives and at the same time motivate the players due to the change in procedures. Repetition is good to a point, after which the players become lazy and lose concentration. On the varsity level emphasis should be on correcting the errors committed rather than continuous repetition of the proper technique prior to the drill period.

According to current motor learning theories an efficient method of learning skills is to space the drills rather than bunch them into ten consecutive practice sessions. This allows for good retention of the skill, improved attention to the task at hand, and permits more time for other areas of equal importance.

CHAPTER TWELVE

Attacking Pressure Zones with the Multiple Set Zone Offense

The use of pressure zones in defensive basketball strategy is increasing every year by leaps and bounds. Television exposure of numerous collegiate and interscholastic basketball games and the success derived from this defensive tactic have influenced thinking in this area greatly. Zone presses are no longer used in only the last few minutes when behind and a team is playing catch-up basketball. It is a definite part and working tool to be utilized at any time of the game to a team's advantage.

At one time small teams who possessed speed, quickness, and stamina were the only ones thought capable of sustaining this type of defense for a major portion of the game. Now there are many types and variations of zone pressure which can be effective. Teams of all sizes can employ zone pressure to a certain extent set down by the limitations of the personnel.

In analyzing zone pressure it is first necessary to understand the primary objectives of the press before evaluating which offensive set and player movement will be most successful in at-

184 *Attacking Pressure Zones with the Multiple Set Zone Offense*

tacking it. Different techniques used by specific zone presses include:

1. Denying the first pass inbounds to panic the passer and gain the ball on a five second violation or rushed pass.
2. Allowing the first pass inbounds and pressuring all outlet lanes to intercept lazy passes.
3. Trapping at the conclusion of a dribble before the player has time to release the ball.
4. Trapping at the time line in back court to take advantage of the ten second time element.
5. Trapping in a corner anywhere on the court to use the boundary lines as an additional defensive aid.
6. Trapping on the side line to force lob passes up court for possible interceptions.
7. Utilizing the ten second clock to advantage by constant harassment in back court.
8. Trapping in the area just over half court bounded by the time line and side line.

In considering the elements of the press, there are three areas of the court in which a zone press can originate from. A press can operate full court and pick the ball up out of bounds immediately under the basket. Second, a press can originate at three-quarter court which is an area between the foul line and top of key. And third, a press can set up as the time line or half court. All presses regardless of origin must either possess an even or an odd front and may or may not have a middle defender. Odd front presses with a middle defender are attacked with the 2-2-1 set. Those without a middle defender (3-2) are attacked with the 2-1-2 set. Even front presses are attacked with the 1-3-1 set. At times the 3-2 set is used to comouflage the movement into the 1-3-1 by shooting a forward up.

Presses can be extremely effective and panic is the single most important element in their success. However, there are certain things that can be done to instill confidence, poise, patience, and team work which are necessary ingredients in defeating zone pressure. Confidence is an element that is gained through practice, repetition, correction, experience, and some prior success. It is imperative that press patterns be covered thoroughly

Attacking Pressure Zones with the Multiple Set Zone Offense 185

and presented frequently in practices and scrimmages to achieve desired results. Players must know what is expected of them and also have experienced the pattern producing the desired results when performed correctly. Poise of players is cemented through practicing and producing the situations that will be presented during a game. Of course, many factors can destroy poise, among them time, score, crowd, court, foul situation, and importance of the contest. Situations must be repeated to simulate game conditions as much as possible in practice sessions to develop both team and individual poise. Some of the methods we use to instill the concept of being patient against a press include:

1. Emphasizing the point that the opponent cannot score when we have the ball.
2. At present there is no time clock in high school basketball limiting the time period in which a shot must be taken.
3. The object is to score more points than the opponent to win. The outcome of the game is not based on the first team scoring a designated number of points being declared the winner.
4. If a situation develops where we are tied up in front court and an imminent jump ball will be the result, we will accept the fact as opposed to throwing an errant pass because we have at least a fifty percent chance of getting it back on the ensuing tap.
5. We emphasize time elements in all practice sessions with the use of a stop watch. All players know exactly how long five seconds can be when passing the ball inbounds. This is done to avoid pushing the panic button and throwing the ball away before the necessary time elapses. We spend a great deal of time on ten second situations in getting the ball over the time line to allow the players thorough knowledge and practical experience in how much time they actually have. Last second shots are timed to gain knowledge in the area of getting off a good percentage shot in a few remaining seconds. Break situations are timed to determine how long it takes to move the ball up the court to secure a good shot.

186 *Attacking Pressure Zones with the Multiple Set Zone Offense*

Finally, teamwork is the most essential element in defeating zone pressure. This is not the time for individual heroics. Many theories have been expressed in this area but there is no one single way for achieving success along this line. One method is to introduce the concept of the word "pact" and related thoughts to explain the importance of teamwork. Pact is defined as an agreement. Teamwork is also an agreement between the five members on the floor to achieve the best possible results that they are capable of. Broken down further to re-emphasize the importance:

P   Pass first to eliminate double team situations from developing

A   Alertness to pick out the open man and the direction from which the trap is developing

C   Concentration is the key to methodical arrangement of players to benefit the offensive attack

T   Togetherness creates offensive openings and possible break situations against double team pressure

One final note concerning teamwork is the basic philosophy of the basketball organization. Teamwork must be emphasized from the first practice and continually made reference to daily in all situations. A team cannot organize their basic offensive attack around one outstanding shooter and expect each member to share the load in pressure situations.

ATTACKING FULL COURT ZONE PRESSURE

The first type of zone pressure to discuss starts operating at full court. Regardless of the setup employed by the defense, the theory behind breaking the press is determined by an odd or even front alignment. Odd front presses generally fall into the categories of a 1-3-1, 3-2, or 1-2-1-1. Even front presses fall into the categories of 2-1-2 or 2-2-1. There are two methods of pressing full court. The press may allow the first pass inbounds before trapping, or the press may attempt to deny the first pass inbounds and hopefully take advantage of five second violations. The major prerequisites for breaking a press involve both ball movement and player movement. Therefore, the eventual working set is moved to each time from the basic 3-2 formation.

The quickest way to beat a press is to take the ball out of bounds quickly before the defense has an opportunity to set up. In this case we instruct the closest player to the ball to take it

Attacking Pressure Zones with the Multiple Set Zone Offense 187

out of bounds immediately. However, many times it is impossible to get the ball inbounds quickly without risking a bad pass. Under these conditions our best passer takes the ball out of bounds on either side of the lane *to prevent the backboard from being an obstruction on the inbounds pass.* The other guard and shortest forward assume positions opposite one another midway between the foul line and endline five feet from the sideline. The remaining forward and center set up at the time line even with the player on his side in the corner. (Diagram 12-4.)

This gives the appearance of a box formation and allows more operating room by staying wide and spreading out the defense. From this formation the offense eventually moves to a 2-2-1 set against an odd front press or a 1-3-1 set against an even front press. Many teams will camouflouge their intentions by aligning with a man-for-man coverage initially. Consequently because of the three-man offensive front the defense will line up likewise in this formation. The key to initiating the pattern is determined by the point defender. If he plays inside the bottom of the foul circle or tight on the ball, a forward breaks quickly to the top of the circle for a direct pass inbounds. The forward breaking up is opposite the ball and is automatically determined by the position of the inbounds passer. (Diagram 12-1.)

The pass is made from 1 to 5. As 5 receives the ball he immediately pivots and faces down court. He has three options available:

1. 5 looks for 4 faking in and breaking deep for a pass if defender D is not staying alert and recovering on the move.

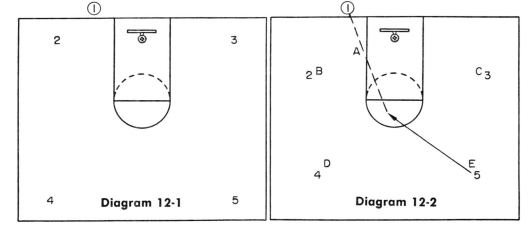

188   *Attacking Pressure Zones with the Multiple Set Zone Offense*

2. 5 looks for the weakside guard (3) streaking down the sideline if 4 is not open.
3. If defender E fails to respond to 5 breaking up for the ball and stays deep to defend, 5 pivots and dribbles down the middle looking for a three on two situation with 3 and 4. The players are instructed to look for any opportunity to break on the press. On many occasions the initial press is broken, moving the ball into forecourt only to hold the ball up until everyone on offense and defense is down court. This actually allows the defense two opportunities to get the ball as they form another defensive pattern over half court. It is our feeling that if the defense is willing to gamble by putting two on one in an attempt to steal the ball, we accept the fact that we will take the opportunity to go to the basket in a three on two or two on one. Diagram 12-3 shows the three options available.

The second phase is automatic and goes into effect immediately if 5 is unable to get a direct pass from 1. There cannot be a delay as a major purpose is to get the ball in play as quickly as possible. Players 2 and 3 fake down court and step back to receive a pass from 1. As soon as 2 receives the ball he immediately looks for 5 at the top of the circle. Should 5's defender leave him and anticipate the trap maneuver on 2, 2 passes quickly to 5 without dribbling. 5 turns and looks for 4 breaking deep or 3 streaking down the sideline. 1 moves to the spot vacated by 3 as a relief measure. (Diagram 12-4.)

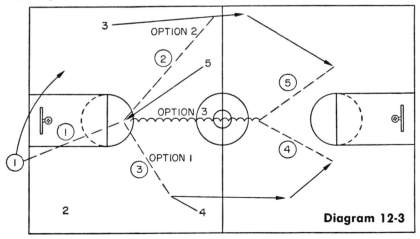

Diagram 12-3

Attacking Pressure Zones with the Multiple Set Zone Offense   189

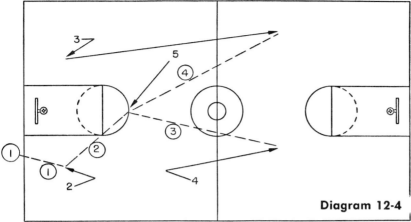

Diagram 12-4

If 2 cannot pass to 5, he looks to midcourt for 4 breaking to the sideline for a pass. As 4 receives the pass, he turns and looks for 3 shooting down the sideline for a baseball pass or 5 who moves up the middle of the court to gain a possible two on one advantage with 3. (Diagram 12-5.)

Some teams will drop their point defender back beyond the foul line to discourage the direct pass from out of bounds to the forward breaking up to the top of the circle. Consequently by playing in front of the forward, it is too risky to attempt a lob pass over the defender especially in back court. The alternate plan of action consists of the forward immediately looping back to his original position if the pass cannot be completed upon his arrival. The pass is then made from 1 to 2 or 3 who have freed themselves by faking down court and stepping back towards the ball. After the inbounds pass, 1 steps inbounds

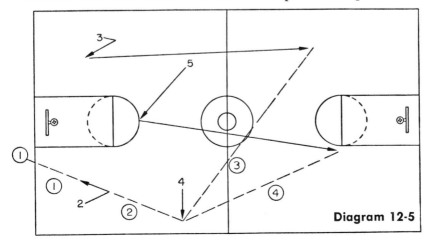

Diagram 12-5

under the basket to become either an outlet for a pass back or a decoy to force the opposite side defender to move over and cover as the double team or trap is forming on the ball. An example will explain this action. 1 passes to 2 and steps inbounds. Defenders A and C close on 2 for the trap. Defender B anticipates a pass back to 1 and moves up to prevent. As B leaves his base position, 3 moves to the top of the circle for a pass from 2 behind the front three defenders. The actual alignment thus becomes a 2-1-2 with 3 in the middle. As soon as 3 has the ball he turns immediately and moves the ball up the middle of the floor. He looks for a deep pass to 4 or 5 slipping behind a defender or a possible three on two situation against defenders D and E if they recover quickly enough to shut off the pass to 4 or 5. We feel confident that 3 can develop a scoring situation on the dribble without placing himself in jeopardy of being double-teamed and having the ball stolen. 3 is one of the better ball handlers on the team and is capable of advancing the ball quickly up the floor on a dribble if necessary to develop an offensive threat. Diagram 12-6 shows the alternate action in breaking a full court zone press.

A final note concerning the time element. Because of the five second allowance to get the ball in play, the offense must respond immediately to the defensive placement of the point defender. This eliminates guesswork. If the point defender is inside the bottom of the foul circle, concentration on a forward breaking up is the primary objective. If the point defender plays beyond the foul line, concentration on getting the ball into play quickly to either guard on the sideline is primary.

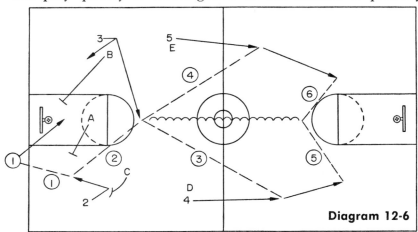

Diagram 12-6

Attacking Pressure Zones with the Multiple Set Zone Offense 191

Some coaches feel that it is a disadvantage to have the entire team operating in the confines of a half court in attempting to break a press. It has been our experience that this approach is most successful and a great deal of teamwork and spirit can be developed. No offensive player is left out of the picture and it makes it very difficult for the defense to double-up and leave a player free. Second, the players enjoy the challenge of attempting to beat the press by out-maneuvering the defender assigned to his area. As mentioned previously, we want to score and prevent the defense a second opportunity to stop us by allowing them to set up once we get the ball over half-court. Percentage-wise if a team can accomplish scoring a basket every two times down the floor against the press, this places a great deal of pressure on the opponent. When considering high school shooting percentages on a whole average between thirty and forty percent, this can develop into a great psychological advantage as well as putting points on the scoreboard.

ATTACKING THREE-QUARTER COURT ZONE PRESSURE

Three-quarter zone pressure originates from a point at approximately the top of the foul circle. The objective of this type of pressure is to force the offense to advance the ball up court to avoid a ten-second violation while in the process attempting variations of traps and double-teaming maneuvers to force a turnover. The defensive appearance can panic a team if they are not ready to operate immediately when the ball is put into play. Pressure at three-quarter court generally takes the form of a 1-3-1, 2-1-2, or 2-2-1 formation. Specific offensive principles are employed to move into the basic press pattern.

1. Against an even front press the offensive set utilized is the 1-3-1.
2. Against an odd front press the offensive set utilized is the 2-2-1.
3. The ball is advanced up the middle of the court against an even front press to draw either defensive guard to the ball. The following pass is to the wing player on the same side that the defender came from.
4. The ball is advanced down either sideline against an odd front press. This draws the defensive point over for a

192   *Attacking Pressure Zones with the Multiple Set Zone Offense*

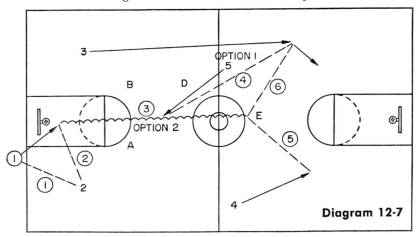

Diagram 12-7

planned trap opening up the other guard for a pass and further available passing lanes before the point can react back.

1-3-1 Set vs 2-2-1 Three-Quarter Court Zone Press

Player 1 takes the ball out of bounds and passes to either 2 or 3 who have assumed a position one step inside the foul line about five feet in from the sideline. Players 4 and 5 take a position even with 2 and 3 one step into forecourt. As soon as 2 or 3 receives the pass, they immediately pass back to 1 stepping inbounds. 1 advances the ball down the middle splitting defenders A and B. As both move to close off 1 from penetrating, either 4 or 5 breaks to a position splitting defenders C and D for a pass. If this can be made, the resultant action is a pass off to the wing man streaking down the sideline beating the deep defenders C and D. The second option is dribbling towards E drawing C and D to close and passing off to a wing man on the sideline or to the other forward who has moved downcourt. (Diagram 12-7.)

A variation exists if either defenders C or D attempt to close off 5 from breaking into the open area to receive a pass. In this case the counter maneuver is for 1 to pass off in the direction that the defender came from to either 2 or 3 sliding behind A or B into the spot vacated by the defensive player C or D who has made a decision to move up. (Diagram 12-8.)

1-3-1 Set vs 2-1-2 Three-Quarter Court Zone Press

1 again advances the ball up the middle to commit either A or B to prevent his penetration. 1 passes off to the wing man

Attacking Pressure Zones with the Multiple Set Zone Offense 193

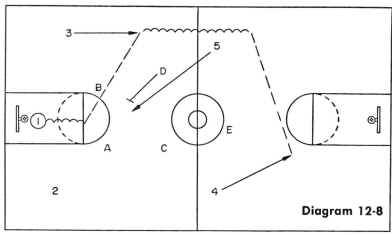

Diagram 12-8

in the direction the defensive guard came from. With the ball in this position either the defensive middle man must move over to cut off the sideline or the defensive forward must commit himself up the sideline to stop penetration. If the defensive middle man moves over, the pass is made to 4 who immediately turns and passes to the opposite wing breaking down the sideline or to 5 dropping deep to the basket. The second alternative is 4 turning and advancing the ball down the middle splitting defenders D and E to form a three on two or dropping a pass off to 2 or 5 moving wide to cover the outside lanes in spreading the defense. (Diagram 12-9.)

If the defensive forward advances up to prevent the sideline penetration by 2, 5 breaks to the sideline ball side to the position vacated by defender E. As 5 receives a pass he immediately looks for 3 breaking deep. (Diagram 12-10.)

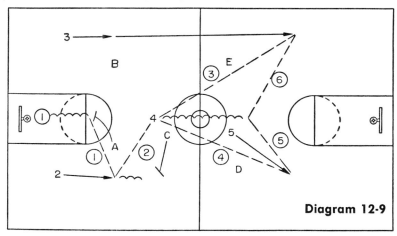

Diagram 12-9

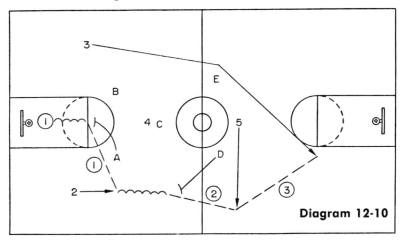

Diagram 12-10

2-2-1 Set vs 1-3-1 Three-Quarter Court Zone Press

The 2-2-1 set keeps the middle clear and allows the forwards to flash into the middle or wide to the sideline depending on the reaction of the defense. Another advantage is that it allows the offensive players an opportunity to slide behind the defense and move back through. This makes it extremely difficult for a defender to trap, cover the player in his area, and be alert for an offensive player sliding in behind him.

The basic movement originates from the 3-2 formation. 1 passes into either 2 or 3. 1 and the receiver of his pass become the two guards in the 2-2-1 setup. The opposite wing becomes a forward and the operative at midcourt on the same side as the receiver of the first inbounds pass becomes the other forward. It is simply a matter of rotating the players depending on the first inbounds pass. (Diagram 12-11.)

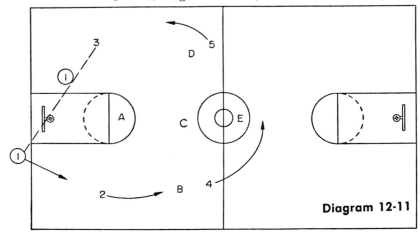

Diagram 12-11

Attacking Pressure Zones with the Multiple Set Zone Offense 195

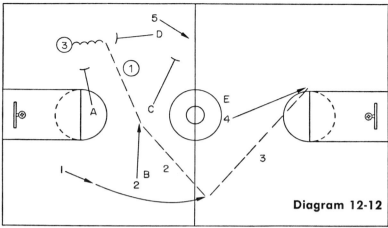

Diagram 12-12

From this formation 3 advances the ball up the sideline drawing the defensive point and wing man over for the trap. 1 remains deep momentarily to provide a release if the next passing options fail to materialize. 3 looks to 4 for a long pass if the defense fails to recover. Second, he looks for 5 up the sideline beyond the defensive trap. If E covers 4 moving downcourt, and C moves over to the sideline anticipating the pass to 5, 2 flashes into the middle area vacated by C looking for a pass. (Diagram 12-12.)

If B moves over to cut off 2 in the middle, the pass is quickly reversed to 1 who passes to 2 looping back out to the sideline. 5 then flashes into the middle looking for a pass if the defense recovers quickly enough to prevent 2 from advancing the ball over half court. (Diagram 12-13.)

This may seem as if there is a great time lapse to reverse the pass back and penetrate from the other side. On the contrary,

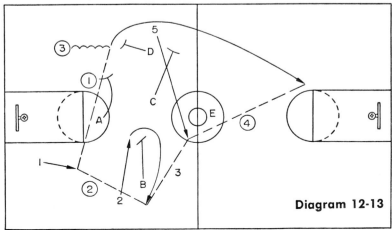

Diagram 12-13

very seldom has a ten-second call been made to prevent us from breaking the press. The main objective is to advance the ball quickly to attack the defense rather than consuming valuable time before getting to the defense. Reversing the pass has also been an advantage in keeping the defense off balance. They become hesitant in their movement and become a little reluctant to expend a total physical effort trapping on the sideline, knowing they might have to move completely across the court to stop the penetration on the other side.

ATTACKING HALF-COURT ZONE PRESSURE

The half-court zone press can be an extremely effective defensive weapon. It originates at the time line and subsequent pressure is applied in all parts of front court. The defense is generally applied as a surprise element, by a team possessing small but quick players that cannot afford the ball moving in close to the basket, or by teams applying their quickness on small courts. The chief asset of this defense is that it disrupts offensive continuity. Pressure is placed on the players to find an opening in a smaller available area. It is important to emphasize the point that when an opening is exploited the players must take immediate advantage of it by producing a good scoring opportunity. Going to the hoop is an often used cliche but is exactly what to do when confronted by this type of defense.

The half-court zone press must eliminate passing lanes to be effective. Therefore, the majority of teams employing a half-court trap press utilize one with a point to prevent ball penetration down the middle. These would include the 3-2, 1-3-1, 3-1-1, or variations of such as a 1-2-1-1 or 1-1-1-2. This form of defense utilizes four major areas to trap the opponent. They are the left midcourt area bounded by the sideline and midcourt line, right midcourt area same, left corner area bounded by the sideline and end line, and the right corner same. The ball is forced away from the middle by the defensive point who forces the ball to be passed or dribbled to the side just over half-court. This maneuver cuts off a return pass to the other guard in back court which would result in an over and back violation. The double-team takes place on the stranded wing man with the remaining three players in the press flooding the passing lanes to intercept any errant passes.

Attacking Pressure Zones with the Multiple Set Zone Offense 197

In breaking the half-court trap press we utilize the 2-2-1 set. The player opposite the ball becomes a temporary high post as he flashes in and out with the ball movement. This allows every offensive player four available passing lanes. With the defense doubling up on the ball the remaining three defenders cannot possibly cover four offensive players. At least one player is clear at all times. The 2-2-1 set is organized with Players 1 and 2 advancing the ball up the floor and providing relief for one another. Players 3 and 4 are the forwards and assume a position one step in from the sideline midway between the foul line and the top of the key. Player 5 is the center and positions himself on the foul lane even with the basket and primarily roams the lane area.

Rule Employment:

1. The guard advancing the ball down the sideline looks immediately to the top of the circle or his sideline for a penetration pass.
2. The guard never dribbles the ball into forecourt initiating a trap and eliminating the other guard as a passing possibility in back court.
3. Once a guard is advancing the ball down the sideline he only passes the ball back to the other guard as the last available passing lane for relief.
4. Whenever the ball is passed into the high post, a back door maneuver is operated with the guard on the same side breaking to the basket. (Diagram 12-14.)

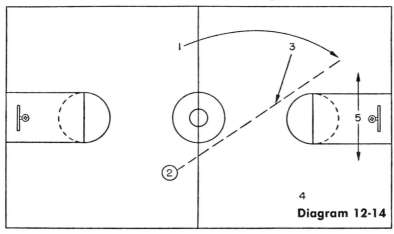

Diagram 12-14

198 Attacking Pressure Zones with the Multiple Set Zone Offense

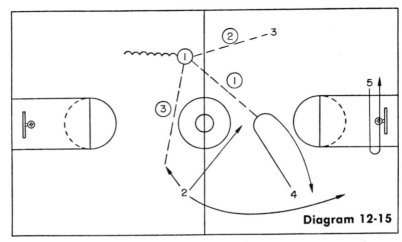

Diagram 12-15

5. Player movement is initiated on every pass to keep the defense from anticipating as much as possible.

The basic sequence of movements to attack the half-court press starts with either 1 or 2 passing inbounds to the other. Either guard advances the ball down quickly while the other guard remains back temporarily for both relief and defensive purposes if a pass is intercepted. 1 moves up to the midcourt line but does not cross over on the dribble. 1 looks for 4 flashing into the middle to initiate a possible back door maneuver. If 4 is not open he moves back to his wing position. 1 then

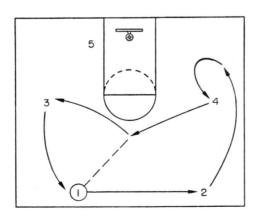

Diagram 12-16

Attacking Pressure Zones with the Multiple Set Zone Offense 19.

looks quickly for 3 down the sideline. If the pass is completed, 2 flashes into the high post and out. If 1 cannot pass to 3, he quickly reverses the pass to 2 who attempts the same penetration passes from the other side. (Diagram 12-15.)

On a back door maneuver without a shot being taken, a simple rotation of players goes into effect. The guard passing in moves to the position vacated by the guard going back door. The forward on the sideline moves out to the guard position same side. The guard on the back door maneuver moves to the forward position vacated by the forward moving into the high post. After the forward in the high post passes out, he moves to the forward position on the opposite side he originally came from. (Diagram 12-16.)

The forward breaking into the middle determines the direction of the rotation, whether it is clockwise or counter-clockwise. During the entire action of the offense the low post or center continuously moves around the lane looking for an opening and a pass.

The second phase of player rotation involves a guard passing to the forward same side and cutting towards the basket. The players rotate to the ball. The forward receiving the ball has four available options. He can give a return pass to the guard cutting through, pass back to the second guard adjusting over to the vacated position, pass to the opposite guard position flashing in to the middle, or pass to the low post moving side on his side and also cutting through. The four peripheral players (both guards and both forwards) perform the rotation with the low post maintaining a position from one side of the lane to the other depending on defensive pressure. (Diagram 12-17.)

SUMMARY

The patterns discussed in attacking full, three-quarter, and half-court zone presses are necessary elements in any successful basketball program. All five players are incorporated to break pressure defenses and consequently offensive pressure is applied as opposed to allowing two or three players attempting to break the press alone. Zone presses can best be beaten by teams willing to go to the basket once the initial pressure is broken.

200   *Attacking Pressure Zones with the Multiple Set Zone Offense*

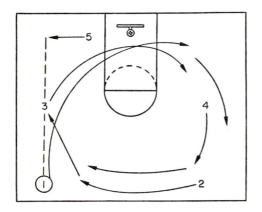

Diagram 12-17

CHAPTER THIRTEEN

Additional Considerations in Instituting the Multiple Set Zone Offense

Evaluating the effectiveness and success of the multiple set zone offense is a difficult task. Although winning is a major factor in determining success, one would be foolish to assume that an offensive system alone or for that matter a particular type of defense is completely responsible for the number of wins a team can compile. Many variables must be considered including available talent, playing experience, practice organization, strength of the league, and the organization of the basketball program along with the dedication of the entire coaching staff at all levels. In analyzing the success that I have had with the multiple set zone offense, it is necessary to trace the steps of its development.

I became head coach at Kenmore West in 1966 and inherited a team that unfortunately had a losing record the previous four seasons. There were a number of obstacles which were present. Team morale was poor. The interest level in basketball was diminishing and the confidence level of the players was extreme-

202 Considerations in Instituting the Multiple Set Zone Offense

ly low. There were two fine starters developed by the former coach returning as the nucleus to build the team. I emphasized fundamentals through constant drilling as the stepping stone to winning basketball and attempted to gain the confidence of the players towards this thinking. I installed a 1-3-1 set as the basic zone offense to simplify offensive thinking as much as possible. We finished the year with a 12-6 record and tied for third in the league. However, I felt we ran into difficulty against a 1-3-1 zone because of our basic offensive pattern. This fact encouraged the formation of the 2-1-2 set specifically designed to operate against the 1-3-1 zone and other odd front defenses. The second season we had two returning starters but injuries hit us often and we finished with a record of 9-9 for fourth place in the league. During the year we experienced difficulty against teams employing a 1-2-2 zone. As we set up in the 2-1-2 set, the defense would drop the point player back in front of the high post. This accomplished a dual purpose of denying the high post the ball as well as matching up with the offensive set. This defensive adjustment frustrated and disrupted the offensive flow. Consequently I introduced a 2-2-1 set by removing the high post and placing him in a low post position to spread the defense as well as opening up the middle. Eventually the 3-2 set was developed for the same reason as well as a basic formation to move into the other sets. The 1-3-1 overload was an outgrowth of the 1-3-1 set actually developed through adjustments by the players. In the straight 1-3-1 set the best shooters were assigned to the wing positions to allow for more area to operate. From this position many times they would move towards the baseline to initiate their penetration movement. Consequently the high and low post players would shift over to become possible scoring threats from a pass if the wing was unable to develop a shot. Because of this I decided to station the post positions on a strongside basis to produce more openings and better passing angles inside. From that point on we established the strongside positioning from either side depending on the shooting abilities of the wing men. We entered the third season with the entire multiple set in operation and two returning starters. Fine play

Considerations in Instituting the Multiple Set Zone Offense 203

by the entire team resulted in a 16-2 record for first place in the league. Only minor adjustments were necessary to fill the positions in the offense. The fourth year began with one returning starter and the final record was 14-4 and our second league championship. The fifth year started with one returning starter and the record duplicated the previous year with a 14-4 record and an unprecedented third straight league championship. I feel strongly that using the multiple set system was a large factor in developing winning consistency. This element along with being fortunate to have players blessed with ability, desire, dedication and pride has made our basketball program a success.

EVALUATION OF PERSONNEL

The evaluation of personnel is extremely important for the success of any offensive pattern. It is necessary to utilize individual special abilities and capabilities as effectively as possible to strengthen offensive movement. Important elements to analyze in making decisions involving proper player placement and utilization in the multiple set offense include:

1. The best passer plays the point position in the odd front sets, is the controlling guard in the even front sets, passes the ball inbounds against full court zone pressure, and advances the ball initially against half and three-quarter court zone pressure.
2. The best shooting guard plays the strongside guard position in the even front sets, and the strongside wing in the odd front sets. This enables a forward who is generally taller, stronger and a little slower to play the weakside wing and be able to get to excellent rebounding position on the offensive boards.
3. The best offensive rebounder plays the low post in the single low post sets and the right low post position in the double low post sets.
4. Certain individuals are adept at pivoting quickly for the fifteen-foot jump shot at the foul line. A high position when holding the ball with a quick and accurate

release along with the knack of working free for the shot are characteristics necessary for this position. A player regardless of size can be extremely effective from the high post if he can perform the above maneuvers.

5. The slowest of the forwards will play in the left low post position in the double low post sets and possibly the weakside wing in the overload. Rebounding and easier access to the basket makes a player of this stature more valuable in his contribution.

All players will not simply fall into a single category for positional placement. Sometimes it will be necessary to hedge somewhat. Give a little somewhere to strengthen the team elsewhere. Generally if the best all around player is a true guard, he should be placed in the strongside wing position. If the best all-around player is a true forward he should play the low post to develop an inside scoring attack.

SET FORMATION

The nature of the multiple set offense dictates that there will be changes in the set formations on the playing floor. There are three methods to designate the desired set. The first involves conveying the information during a timeout to the entire team. Of course, the information should basically be established prior to the game in the practice sessions getting ready for the opponent. The second method involves a change on the floor and the information can be given to the captain at the sideline during a foul shooting situation. The third method is to relay the information to the floor leader from the bench by the use of hand signals. A simple order would include one finger designating the 1-3-1 set, two fingers designating the 2-1-2 set, three fingers designating the 3-2 set, 4 fingers designating the 2-2-1 set, and an open hand designating the 1-3-1 overload set. Depending on which set is signaled for, the strongside is designated by the appropriate hand. An example would be the overload set strongside left being signaled with the left hand raised and open.

Sometimes the offense may want to camouflage the true in-

Considerations in Instituting the Multiple Set Zone Offense 205

tention by organizing in the 3-2 set and rotating to the actual set desired to cause missed assignments by the defense. Diagrams 10-3 to 10-6 in the section devoted to defeating the match-up zone in Chapter Ten illustrate the movement necessary to rotate to the various sets from the 3-2 formation. The rotation can be clockwise or counter-clockwise depending on which direction the point player dribbles (left or right) or is forced by the defense. Below is a chart formed through experience to select the proper sets against different zone defenses.

Zone Defense Employed	Pre-Opponent Concentration	Most Effective Set
3-2	1-3-1 2-1-2 Overload	2-1-2
	1-3-1 2-1-2 Overload	2-1-2
2-1-2	1-3-1 Overload 2-2-1	1-3-1
2-3	Overload 3-2 2-1-2	3-2
1-3-1	2-2-1 Overload 3-2	2-2-1
2-2-1	Overload 1-3-1 2-1-2	1-3-1

IMPLICATION OF STATISTICS

Statistical information can be extremely valuable in evaluating the success of a basketball program. Depending on the values of the coach success can be measured in terms of wins and losses, player improvement and standing in various categories, team improvement and standing in various categories, ability to place players in colleges, and comparison of past teams and individuals. Statistical information can be recorded in terms of individual totals, team totals, individual records, and team records. They can be kept as pre-season scrimmage stats, game stats, total stats of individuals and the team for the year, and basketball records at the school.

I believe strongly in the value of statistics. It is a great motivator for players. Players like to know how well they are doing, how they compare with other team members, the amount of improvement from game to game, and how they compare with the records of former players. Statistics can also reveal the most effective sets for the available personnel along with specific placing of personnel in certain positions. Subjective judgment by the coach is kept to a minimum in determining the starting lineup and top line substitutes as the players can see in black and white their performance and who the most consistent players on the team are.

TERMINOLOGY

In any basketball program organization is instrumental in achieving success. The cooperation between the head coach, assistant coach, and ninth grade coach is necessary. I am fortunate to have fine assistants who contribute greatly to the overall success through their cooperation, loyalty, and effort. One important item that has a tendency to be overlooked is in the area of terminology. It may seem insignificant but in the long run contributes to learning efficiency by the players. Players at times will neglect asking questions to clarify certain things for fear of looking bad in front of the rest of the team. Consequently much can be lost in the translation from coach to player. Sometimes it can delay learning, other times it can cost a ball game. Every coach has certain terms to describe pet situations or maneuvers. The definitions may differ from coach to coach. If the differences exist from level to level, confusion may result in the players. Therefore, it is important that all

Considerations in Instituting the Multiple Set Zone Offense 207

coaches in the basketball program use the same terminology in describing offensive and defensive strategy.

GAME STRATEGY

As each game is approached, a specific game plan must be organized. Among the essential items is the offensive preparation to attack the opposing team's defensive setups. This would include the choice of sets to emphasize, the options to be used, specific player position, special team considerations, and a player depth chart.

The selection of sets to use revolves around the type of zone defense employed. Once the sets have been decided upon, the most effective options to use are considered. The players are assigned to their specific positions. However, certain players may be capable of using their talents in other positions. Some players are capable of operating equally effectively from two positions and are known as swing players. This might involve high-low post ability, guard-wing ability, or low post-wing ability. This is important information to have in making player adjustments. Next it is necessary to include special team considerations. At times situations will develop in which the personnel assigned on the court cannot generate a scoring thrust, keep the continuity of the pattern running, obtain second efforts on the offensive board, hit consistently from the floor, recover quickly on defense, or handle defensive pressure. A valuable item to have is a listing of various combinations of players capable of getting the job done and correcting the existing weakness on the floor. Finally, a depth chart is essential for the players' knowledge and unexpected occurrences. Injury, illness, foul trouble, or other factors make it impossible for a player to continue. Player replacement information should be prepared beforehand and be at the fingertips to utilize when needed.

PRACTICE GUIDELINES

Time is the most important single factor in developing the multiple set zone offense. The material must not be rushed, but

208   *Considerations in Instituting the Multiple Set Zone Offense*

introduced gradually to assure proper learning to take place. There are certain steps to follow in aiding the learning process. The first set introduced is the 3-2 with all available options. Explanation, demonstration, participation, and dummy work follow. A defense performing token resistance follows and then full go. Next the various zones which will necessitate its use and the vulnerabilities of each are concentrated on. Repetition and review will cement the concepts. The next set introduced by the same fashion is the 1-3-1. The adjustment will easily be seen as a low post moves high to become the high post player. The same procedure of learning the set movement is conducted. The third set to follow is the 1-3-1 overload in which the major adjustment is moving the high and low post to a tight position on the lane left or right designating the strongside. The fourth set to develop is the 2-2-1 set and related options. Finally the 2-1-2 set with the deep offensive player moving to a high post and both wing men dropping to the double low post positions.

After familiarity is developed with each individual set, similarity of movement is introduced to simplify the basic action, the cutter in the sets without a high post being the second man from the corner and the cutter in the sets with a high post being the first man from the corner. The roll maneuver is constructed in the same fashion. The next stage involves set reaction by the players to the coach's signal. At first the set is formed only by a hand signal. As mentioned previously in relaying information to the floor this can be done by the use of fingers. The other hand indicates the particular option. An open hand is the passing option. A closed fist indicates the roll option. An open hand with a slicing motion indicates the cutter option. An example to explain this would be the left hand open, right hand closed fist. This would signify to run the roll option from the 1-3-1 overload strongside left. The signals are only used in situations where a specific play is to be run, otherwise the normal continuity of the set will be used after the set designation by the coach. However, it is good practice for the players to receive visual stimulation and to respond accordingly as a unit. Following the introduction and learning of the

Considerations in Instituting the Multiple Set Zone Offense 209

movement pattern in the multiple set system, breakdown drills previously mentioned in Chapter Nine are used to improve timing and execution. A final stage of preparation involves pre-season scrimmages with other schools. Scrimmages should be set up according to the type of defenses that will be seen in league play to afford the opportunity to sharpen all parts of the multiple set zone offense.

Index

A

Adjustments, combat combination defenses. 143-162 (*see also* Combination defenses)
Advantages, 13-21 (*see also* Principles)
Aggressive layup drill, 174-175
Ahead or behind, 17
Airborne layup drill, 177-178
Alternating box and 1 defense, 155-156
Arm, hack, 173
Around the horn, 171-172
Automatic maneuvers:
  body position drill, 96
  cutting and reversing, 90-91
  developing the second effort, 97-98
  faking and penetrating, 92, 94-95
  introduction, 87-88
  momentary delay drill, 96-97
  penetrating the baseline, 92
  releasing and moving, 89-90
  reversing the pass, 88-89
  shooting and following, 95-97
  shot reaction drill, 97

B

Backline zone, 139-140
Balance, floor, 122-123

Ball position, 166
Baseline, penetrating, 92
Behind, ahead or, 17
Body position, 166
Body position drill, 96
Box and 1 defense, 145-148, 148-151
Breakdown drills:
  cut and reverse maneuver, 109
  faking and penetrating points, 111-112
  introduction, 99-100
  offensive cutting action, 102-105
  perimeter passing, 100-102
  post options, 105-109
  reversing the passing action, 109-111
  summary, 112

C

Close shots, playing for, 113-114
Combination defenses:
  double forward movement vs triangle and 2 defense, 160-161
  double guard movement vs triangle and 2 defense, 157-158
  2-1-2 perimeter set, 158
  2-2-1 weakside slide set, 157-158
  forward option vs box and 1 defense, 148-151

Index

Combination defenses: *(cont.)*
 1-3-1 cut and roll set, 149
 1-3-1 overload set, 149, 151
 3-2 baseline screen set, 148-149
 forward option vs diamond and 1 defense, 153-155
  1-3-1 overload set, 155
  2-1-2 perimeter set, 153-154
  2-2-1 weakside slide set, 154
 guard-forward movement vs triangle and 2 defense, 159-160
  1-3-1 overload set, 159
  2-2-1 weakside slide set, 159-160
 guard option vs box and 1 defense, 145-148
  1-3-1 cut and roll set, 147
  1-3-1 overload set, 148
  3-2 baseline screen set, 145-147
 guard option vs diamond and 1 defense, 151-153
  1-3-1 overload set, 152-153
  2-1-2 perimeter set, 151
  2-2-1 weakside slide set, 151
 player movements vs alternating box and 1 defense, 155-156
 summary, 161-162
Committing the defense, 30
Commitment, 21
Concentration, 167
Confidence:
 level, 201
 player, 15
Confusion, 206
Contact drill, 172-173
Continuity, 17
Corner trap, 127-129
Cut and reverse maneuver, 109
Cutting action, offensive, 102-105
Cutting and reversing, 90-91
Cutter option, 64, 67-69, 71-72, 75-76, 79-80, 83-84

D

Dedication, 201
Defensive point, 14
Defensive theory, 23
Definitions, 206
Diamond and 1 defense, 151-153, 153-155
Double forward movement vs triangle and 2 defense, 160-161
Double guard, 45
Double guard movement vs triangle and 2 defense, 157-158
Double low post exchange, 55-57
Double low post players, 45
Double-team layup drill, 175-176

Double teaming, 23
Down the middle layup drill, 175
Dribble, penetrating on, 31-32
Drilling, constant, 202
Drills:
 aggressive layup, 174-175
 airborne layup, 177-178
 around the horn, 171-172
 body position, 96
 breakdown, 99-112
  (see also Breakdown drills)
 contact, 172-173
 cut and reverse maneuver, 109
 double team layup, 175
 down the middle layup, 175
 faking and penetrating points, 111-112
 5-10-15, 173-174
 hack on arm, 173
 jab stomach, 173
 jumping layup, 176-177
 knudge hip, 173
 loose ball layup, 175
 man in middle passing, 180
 momentary delay, 96-97
 offensive cutting action, 102-105
 pass and press, 170-171
 perimeter passing, 100-102, 179
 post options, 105-109
 quick release, 169-170
 reversing the passing action, 109-111
 shot reaction, 97
 shooting, 169-181
 slap on wrist, 173
 split the offense, 180-181
 spot shooting, 172
 two man tapping, 177
 two on one passing, 178
 zig zag passing, 179-180

E

Evaluation, personnel:
 best all-around player, 204
 offensive rebounder, 203
 passer, 203
 pivoting for 15-foot jump shot at foul line, 203
 shooting guard, 203
 slowest of forwards, 204
 special abilities and capabilities, 203
 strongside wing position, 204
Even front zones, 14
Exchanges:
 double low post, 55-57
 low post — high post, 53-55
Experience, playing, 201

F

Faking and penetrating, 92, 94-95
Faking and penetrating points, 111-112
Fast break, 13
Feeder, 37
Field goal, made or missed, 17
5-10-15 drill, 173-174
Flexibility, 17, 19
Floor balance, maintaining, 122-123
Following, shooting and, 95-97
Formations, 64, 204-205
Forward option:
    box and 1 defense, vs, 148-151
    diamond and 1 defense, vs, 153-155
Foul shot, made or missed, 17
Fouls, 13, 14
Fronting pressure on the low post, 134-135
Fronting pressure on the high post, 133-134
Frontline zone, 140-141
Full court, 186-191

G

Game strategy, 207
Going to the hoop, 196
Guard-forward movement vs triangle and
    2 defense, 159-160
Guard option:
    box and 1 defense, vs, 145-148
    diamond and 1 defense, vs, 151-153

H

Hack on the arm, 173
Half-court zone pressure, 196-199
High post:
    options, 48-50
    player, 41-42
    relieving fronting pressure, 133-134
Hip, knudge, 173

I

Index, shooting, 163-166
Inside rotation, 60-61
Interest level, 201
Interior attack:
    double low post exchange, 55-57
    effectiveness, 47
    high post options, 48-50
    inside rotation, 60-61
    introduction, 47-48
    low post flash, 60
    low post-high post exchange, 53-55
    low post loop, 57-58
    low post options, 50-53

Interior attack: *(cont.)*
    low post roll, 59
    summary, 61-62
    weakside sift, 60

J

Jab at the stomach, 173
Jump switching, 23
Jumping layup drill, 176-177

K

Knudge the hip, 173

L

Lane area, mobility in, 37
League, strength, 201
Loose ball layup drill, 175
Low post:
    flash, 60
    loop, 57-58
    options, 50-53
    position, 42-43
    relieving fronting pressure, 134-135
    roll, 59
Low post-high post exchange, 53-55

M

Man in the middle passing drill, 180
Maneuvers, automatic, 87-98 *(see also*
    Automatic maneuvers)
Matchup zone, 135-139
Midcourt pressure, 129-131
Middle sag, 131-133
Mismatch, 24
Mobility in lane area, 37
Momentary delay drill, 96-97
Morale, team, 201
Moving, releasing and, 89-90

O

Odd front zones, 14
Offensive:
    cutting action, 102-105
    pressures, 23-34 *(see also* Pressures,
        offensive)
    strategy, 112-125 *(see also* Strategy)
Offensive patterns, 63-86 *(see also*
    Patterns)
One man front, 14
1-3-1 cut and roll set, 64, 66-69, 147, 149
1-3-1 overload set, 64, 81-85, 148, 149, 151,
    152-153, 155, 159

Index

213

1-3-1 set, 192-193
1-3-1 three-quarter court zone press, 194-196
Options:
cutter, 64, 67-69, 71-72, 75-76, 79-80, 83-84
forward, 148-151, 153-155
guard, 145-148, 151-153
high post, 48-50
low post, 50-53
passing, 64, 66-67, 70, 73-75, 77-79, 81-82
post, 105-109
post or roll maneuver, 64-65, 69, 72-73, 76-77, 80-81, 84-85
selection against situation zones, 127-142
(see also Situation zones)
Outside shooting team, 14
Overloading, 18
Overloading a side, 33
Overshifting defense, 123-124

P

Pact, 186
Pass and press drill, 170-171
Pass, reversing, 88-89
Passing:
moving, 19
option, 64, 66-67, 70, 73-75, 77-79, 81-82
perimeter, 100-102
triangles, 24-26
Passing lane denial, 133
Patience on offense, 122
Patterns:
execution, 33-34
five formations, 64
introduction, 63-65
offensive, 63-86
1-3-1 Cut and Roll, 66-69
cutter option, 67-69
passing option, 66-67
roll option, 69
1-3-1 Overload, 81-85
cutter option, 83-84
passing option, 81-82
roll option, 84-85
rotating, 17-18
summary, 85-86
3-2 Baseline Screen, 73-77
cutter, 75-76
passing options, 73-75
roll option, 76-77
2-1-2 Perimeter, 70-73
cutter, 71-72
passing option, 70
roll option, 72-73
2-2-1 Weakside Slide, 77-81
cutter option, 79-80

Patterns: *(cont.)*
passing option, 77-79
roll option, 80-81
Penetrating:
baseline, 92
dribble, 31-32
faking and, 92, 94-95
points, 111-112
Penetration, 18-19
Percentage shooting, 114-117, 168
Perimeter attack, 47
Perimeter passing, 100-102
Perimeter passing drill, 179
Personnel evaluation:
best all-around player, 204
offensive rebounder, 203
passer, 203
pivoting for 15-foot jump shot at foul line, 203
shooting guard, 203
slowest of forwards, 204
strongside wing position, 204
Personnel, placement, 35-45 *(see also* Positions)
Placement, personnel, 35-45 *(see also* Positions)
Player movement vs alternating box and 1 defense, 155-156
Players:
analysis, 36-39
confidence, 15
double guard, 45
double low post, 45
executing offensive pattern, 38
following shot effectively, 36
high post, 41-42
low post, 42-43
mobility in lane area, 37
offensive rebounding position, 37
placement, 35-45 *(see also* Positions)
point, 39-41
reaction under pressure, 39
responsibility and obligation, 38-39
scorer or feeder, 37
spot shooter, 36-37
"take charge" attitude, 38
transition from offense to defense, 37
wing, 43-44
Point position, 39-41
Positional strengths, 15-16
Positions:
double guard, 45
double low post, 45
high post, 41-42
introduction, 35-36
low post, 42-43
player analysis, 36-39

214   *Index*

Positions: *(cont.)*
   execution of offensive pattern, 38
   following shot effectively, 36
   good offensive rebounding position, 37
   mobile in lane area, 37
   reaction under pressure, 39
   responsibility and obligation, 38-39
   scorer or feeder, 37
   spot shooter, 36-37
   "take charge" attitude, 38
   transition from offense to defense, 37-38
  point, 39-41
  wing, 43-44
Post maneuver, 64
Post options, 105-109
Practice guidelines:
  aiding learning process, 208
  breakdown drills, 209
  cutter option, 208
  execution, 209
  1-3-1, 208
  1-3-1 overload, 208
  passing option, 208
  pre-season scrimmages with other
    schools, 209
  relaying information to floor, 208
  roll maneuver, 208
  roll option, 208
  set reaction by players to coach's
    signal, 208
  signals, 208
  similarity of movement, 208
  3-2 with all available options, 208
  time, 207, 209
  2-1-2 set, 208
  2-2-1 set and related options, 208
  visual stimulation, 208
Practice, organization, 201
Pressure:
  reaction under, 39
  types, 23
Pressure zones:
  break situations, 185
  confidence, 184
  full court, 186-191
    ball movement, 186
    ball out of bounds quickly, 186
    box formation, 187
    deny first pass inbounds, 186
    drop point defender, 189
    first pass inbounds before trapping, 186
    five unable to get direct pass from 1, 188
    if 2 can't pass to 5, 189
    key to initiating pattern, 187
    odd or even, 186
    1-3-1, 186, 187
    1-2-1-1, 186

Pressure zones: *(cont.)*
    pass from 1 to 5, 187-188
    player movement, 186
    point defender, 187
    take advantage of five second viola-
      tions, 186
    3-2, 186
    two methods, 186
    2-1-2, 186, 190
    2-2-1, 186, 187
  half-court, 196-199
    back door maneuver, 198-199
    chief asset, 196
    eliminate passing lanes, 196
    going to the hoop, 196
    1 or 2 passing inbounds to other, 198
    originates, 196
    rotation, 199
    surprise element, 196
    trap the opponent, 196
  introduction, 183-186
  many types and variations, 183
  pact, 186
  panic, 184
  patience, 184, 185
  personnel, limitations, 183
  philosophy of basketball organization, 186
  poise. 184
  primary objectives, 183
  rule employment, 197-199
  success derived, 183
  summary, 199-200
  teamwork, 184, 186
  techniques, 184
  television, 183
  three areas of court, 184
  three-quarter court, 191-196
    moving into basic press pattern, 191-192
    objective, 191
    1-3-1 set vs 2-1-2, 192-193
    1-3-1 set vs 2-2-1, 192
    originates, 191
    principles, 191
    2-2-1 set vs 1-3-1, 194-196
  time clock, 185
  time elements, 185, 190
  rise, 183
Pressures, offensive:
  committing the defense, 30
  emphasizing pattern execution, 33-34
  employing weakside action, 27-29
  introduction, 23-24
  mismatch, creating, 24
  overloading a side, 33
  passing triangles, utilizing, 24-26
  penetrating on dribble, 31-32
  screening the zone, 29-30

Index

215

splitting the defense, 27
Principles:
  advantages of zone defense, 13-14
  ahead or behind, 17
  against poor outside shooting team, 14
  changing defenses, 17
  concentrating on offensive ability, 14
  confidence, player, 15
  constant rebounding position, 13
  continuity, player, 17
  decreasing fouls, 14
  defensive point, 14
  disrupting defensive plans, 20
  even front zones, 14
  fast break after rebound, 13
  forcing defensive commitment, 21
  made or missed field goal, 17
  odd front zones, 14
  offensive advantage, 16-17
  one man front, 14
  overloading, 18
  passing and moving, 19
  penetrating defense, 18-19
  positional strengths, 15-16
  protecting star player, 13
  rotating the pattern, 17-18
  score, 17
  spreading defense, 19
  tempo of game, 14
  time out period, 17
  time remaining, 17
  two man front, 14
  utilizing big men, 13
  utilizing individual strengths, 20-21
  variation in offensive attack, 19-20
  zone awareness, 14-15
Program, organization, 201

Q

Questions, 206
Quick release, 167
Quick release drill, 169-170

R

Range, shooting, 167-168
React, ability to, 14
Rebounding position, constant, 13
Release, quick, 167
Releasing and moving, 89-90
Reversing, cutting and 90-91
Reversing the pass, 88-89
Reversing the passing action, 109-111
Roll maneuver, 64, 69, 72-73, 76-77, 80-81, 84-85

Rotating, pattern, 17-18
Rotation, inside, 60-61

S

Sag, middle, 131-133
Score, 17
Scorer, 37
Scouting reports, 20
Screening the zone, 29-30
Second efforts, 23, 97-98
Set formation, 204-205
Shooting, 23, 95-97, 163-181
Shot reaction drill, 97
Situation zones, 127-141
Size, 23
Slap on the wrist, 173
Split the offense drill, 180-181
Splitting the defense, 27
Spot shooter, 36-37
Spot shooting drill, 172
Spreading the defense, 19
Statistics, 205-206
Strategy, 113-125
Strengths, 15-16, 20-21

T

Terminology, 206
Three-quarter court, 191-196
3-2 baseline screen set, 64, 73-77, 145-147, 148-149
Trap, corner, 127-129
Trapping, 23, 127-129
Triangle and 2 defense, 157-158, 159-160, 160-161
Triangles, passing, 24-26
Two man trapping drill, 177
2-1-2 perimeter set, 64, 70-73, 151, 153-154, 158, 160-161
Two on one passing drill, 178
2-1-2 three-quarter court zone press, 192-193
2-2-1 set, 194, 196
2-2-1 three-quarter court zone press, 192
2-2-1 weakside slide set, 64, 77-81, 152, 154, 157-158, 159-160

W

Weak areas of zones, attacking, 117-121
Weakside action, 27-29
Weakside sift, 60
Wing players, 43-44

Z

Zig zag passing drill, 179-180